DEAD FUNNY

PUNCH among the Angels

Edited by Peter Barnes

A PUNCH BOOK
Published in association with
GRAFTON BOOKS
A Division of the Collins Publishing Group

LONDON GLASGOW
TORONTO SYDNEY AUCKLAND

Grafton Books
A Division of the Collins Publishing Group
8 Grafton Street, London W1X 3LA

Published by Grafton Books 1987

British Library Cataloguing in Publication Data

Dead Funny : Punch among the angels
1. Death – Caricatures and cartoons
2. English wit and humor, Pictorial
I. Barnes, Peter, *1946* – II. Punch
741.5'942 NC1476

ISBN 0-246-13241-8

Printed in Great Britain by
William Collins Sons & Co. Ltd, Glasgow

Introduction

Though amateur photographers and home-video buffs are ever eager to make a visual record of most major life events, there seems to be an unwritten rule that death should go unrecorded. Every family has its collection of photographs of milestones – newborn babies, birthday parties, weddings, anniversaries – but very few consider it seemly to snap the last breath or the arrival of the hearse at the crematorium, and fewer still frame their efforts and display them on the sideboard.

Punch cartoonists are less restrained. While other artists depict the great and the good as they shuffle off this mortal coil, whether it be in the bath *à la* Marat, or falling off the bed like Chatterton, the humble cartoonist is content with recording more mundane ends. Albert's unsuccessful cook hangs herself on her own *fondue*; Duncan's ventriloquist's dummy continues to speak despite its master's demise; and Noel Ford treats us to a variety of send-offs, from the motor cycle display team stacked in death as in life, to the punk being moved closer to his maker in a dustbin inscribed RIP.

Mark Twain may have concluded that there was no humour in heaven, but it's a belief that is not shared by *Punch* cartoonists; being game for a laugh appears to be a requirement for new arrivals at the Pearly Gates. Unless, of course, as de la Nougerede reminds us, one is a plumber, when all entrance requirements are automatically waived. Once in, you know you've arrived by the abundance of clouds. For the cartoonist, clouds bring the benefit of not having to draw feet, an advantage quickly wiped out by the requirement to add wings. These wings, however, facilitate numerous flights of fancy. Bill Stott's heaven is served by public telephones that all work. For Heath, TV quiz shows have Shakespeare, Beethoven and Einstein on the team. And Schwadron has the male partner of a heavenly reunited couple remind his wife that the wedding vows were only valid until death, as he sets off with his arm round a younger and prettier angel. Even Mark Twain receives his come-uppance at the pen of Henry Martin when a celestial celebrity roast is organised in his honour, presumably to encourage him to eat his own words.

Depictions of heaven outnumber those of the other place by about four to one, though whether this is a reflection of the saintly life led by cartoonists or the desire of the Art Editor to keep on the right side of *Punch*'s large clerical readership I am in no position to judge. What may be lacking in quantity is more than made up for in satanic quality. Banx's little devils impersonate the Samaritans at a subterranean switchboard, while in another quarter of the underworld flames lick around the serried ranks of McLachlan's damned, condemned to an eternity of Space Invaders machines.

This introduction is in grave danger of becoming depressing. Quick, turn the page, enter the Pearly Gates, and feast on the ambrosia within. But stop short of dying with laughter.

Peter Barnes
February 1987

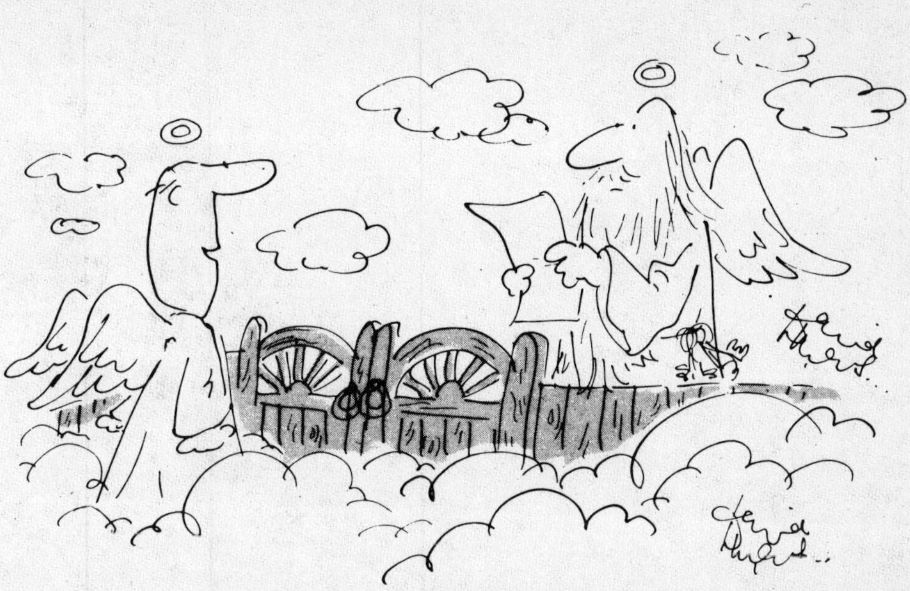

"To tell the truth – I always thought they'd be more pearly."

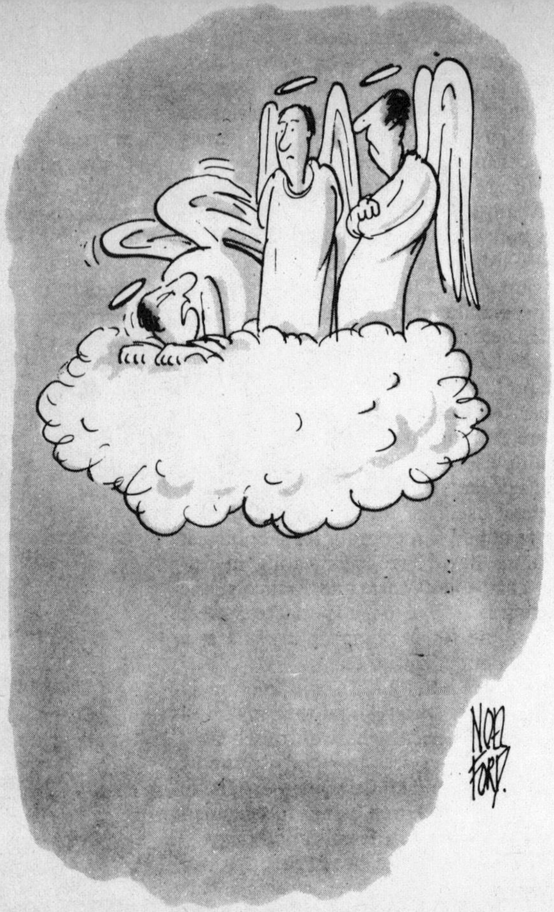

"I was scheduled for the other place, but the bastards found out about my fear of heights."

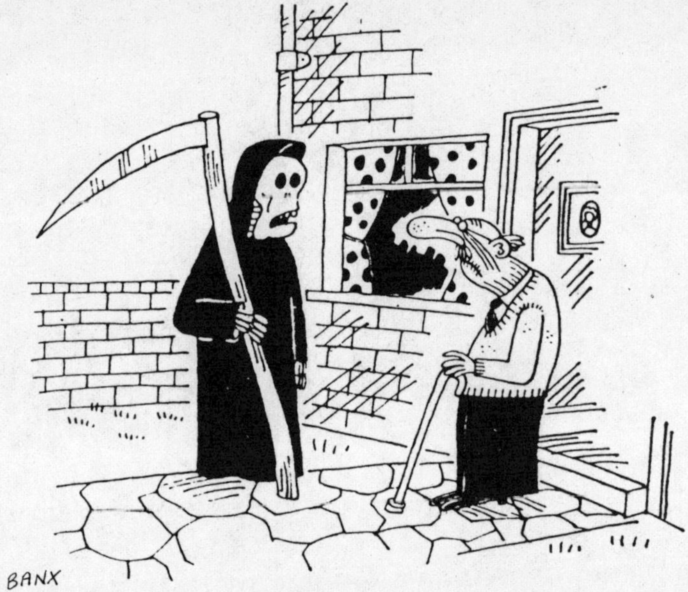

"I thought you'd like to know – you've been pencilled in for next Tuesday."

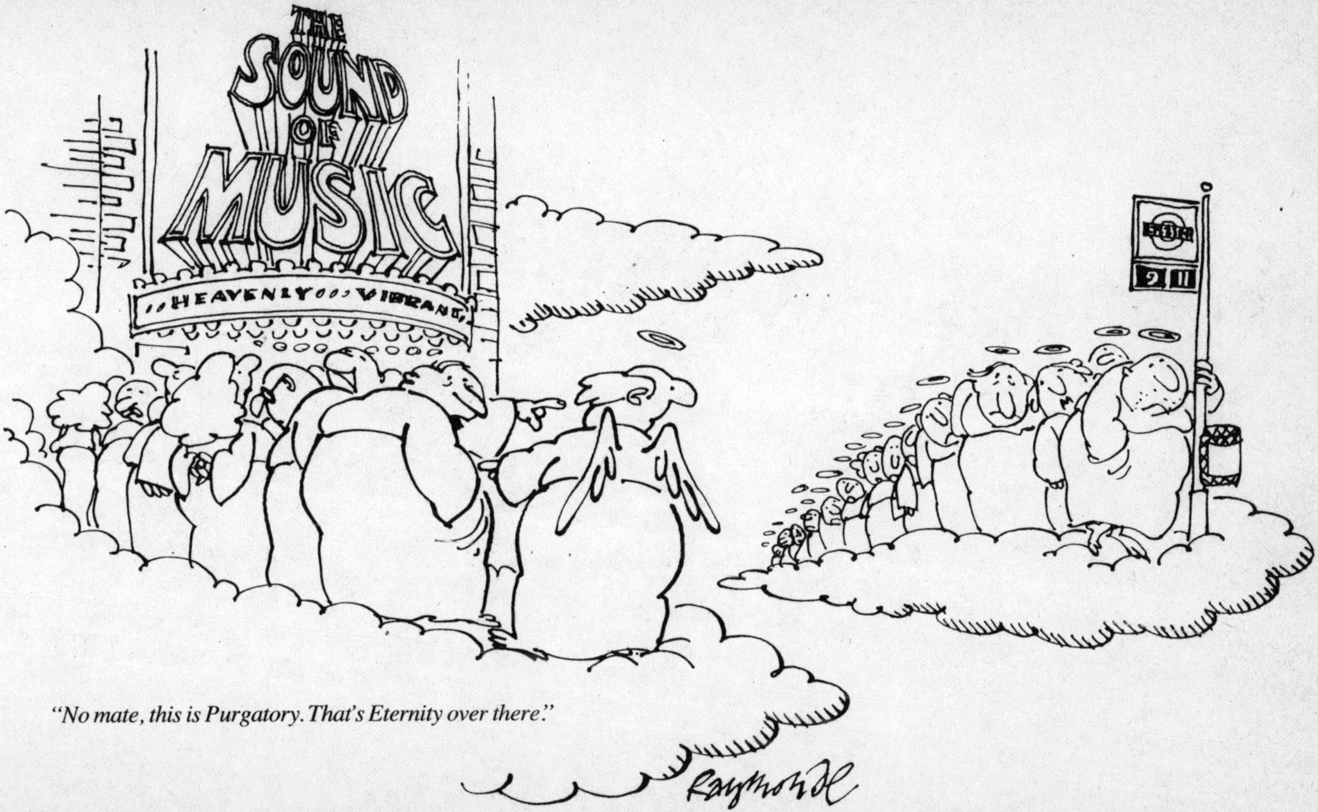

"No mate, this is Purgatory. That's Eternity over there."

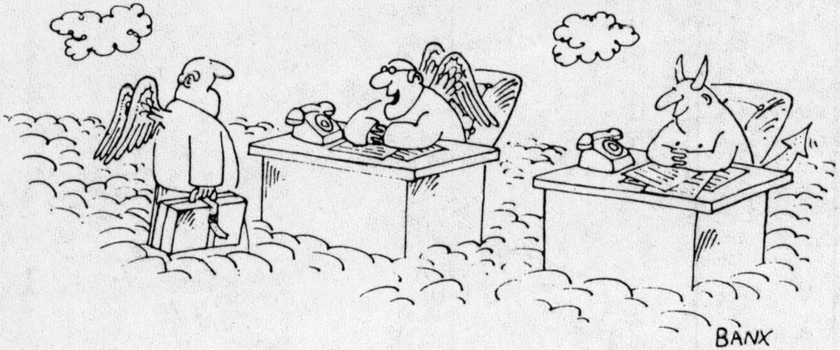

"**I** deal with tax avoidance – **he** deals with tax evasion."

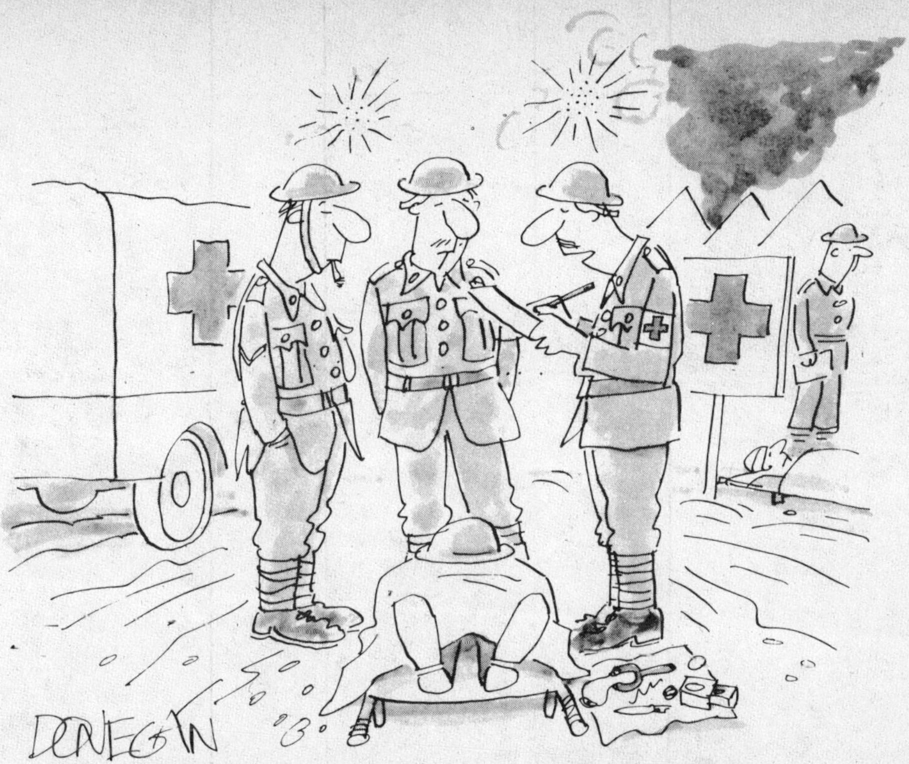

"Personal effects – one bit of string, one conker, one broken-bladed penknife, one catapult, one dead beetle in matchbox and one half-sucked gobstopper. Not much for a General, is it?"

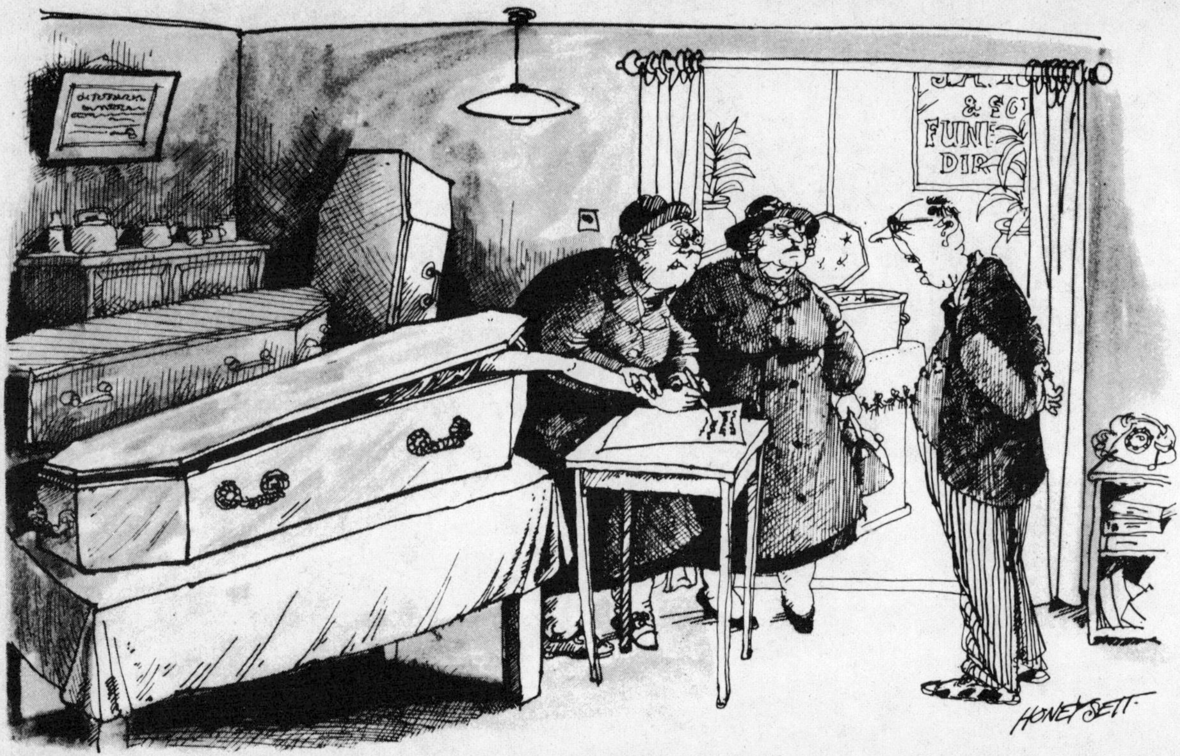

"Just because it's in his own hand, Mrs Figmarsh, doesn't automatically make it a legal will."

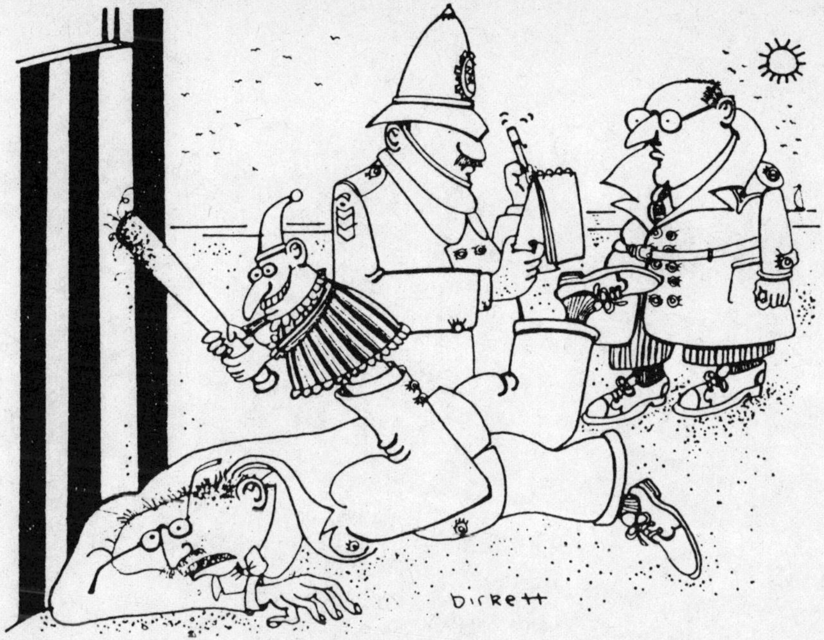

"Personally, Sergeant, I'd say suicide – but I think we're going to need a psychiatrist's report."

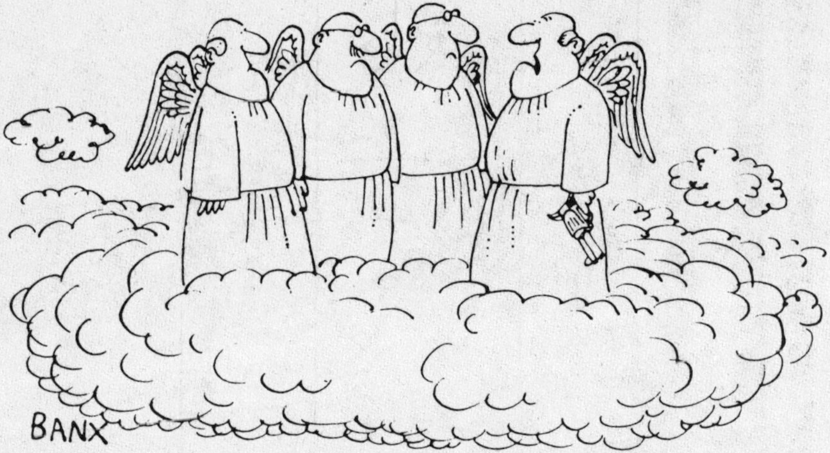

"Russian roulette, Russian roulette! Doesn't anyone know any other games?"

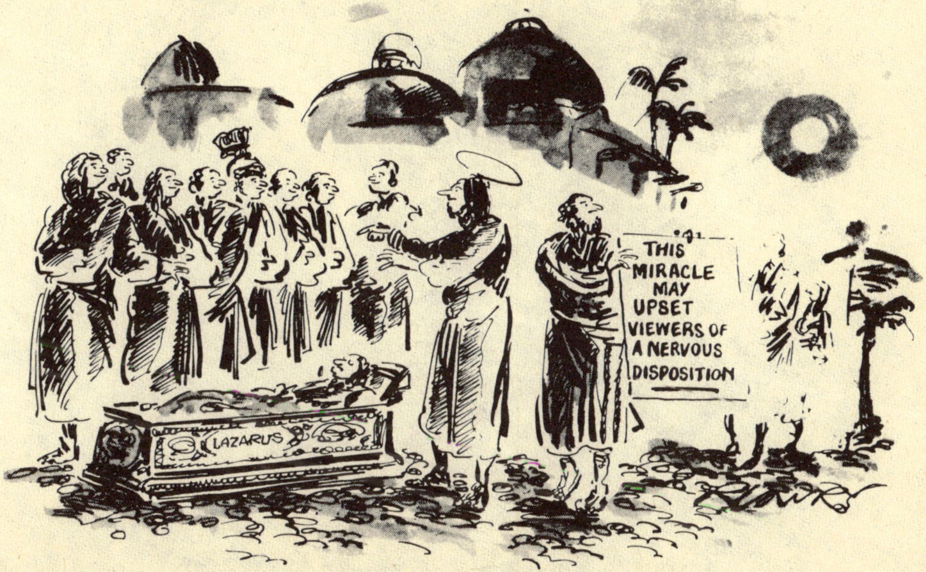

LAZARUS
THIS MIRACLE MAY UPSET VIEWERS OF A NERVOUS DISPOSITION

"The family's never going
to get over this."

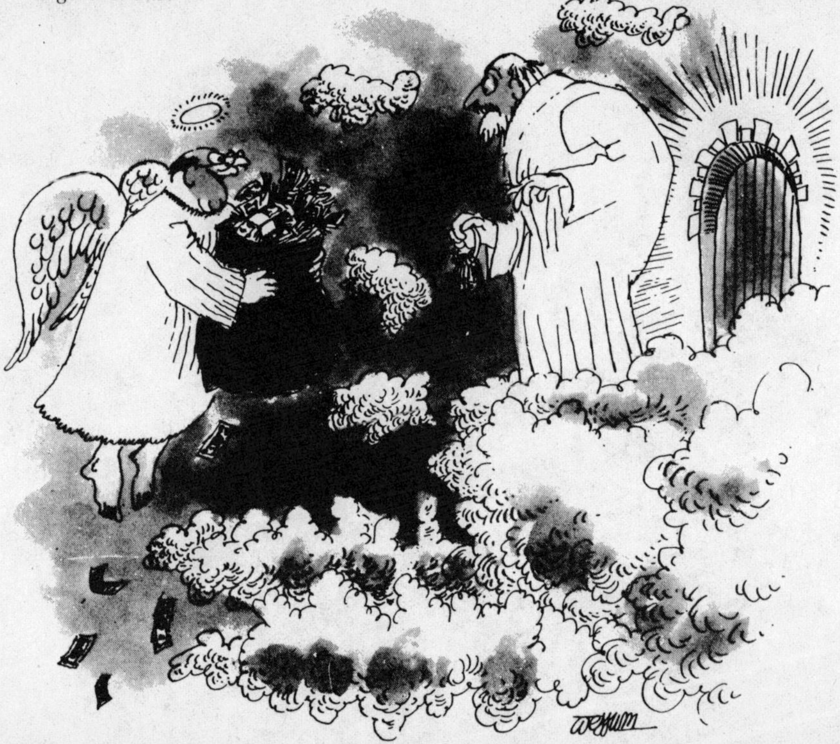

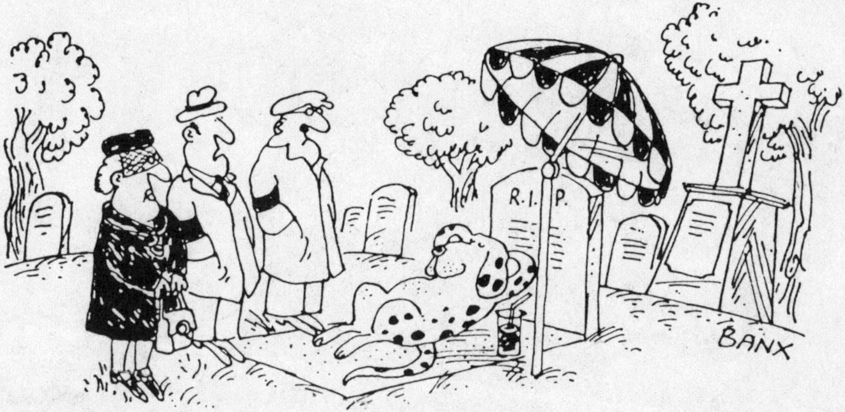

"I didn't think the dog would take it so well".

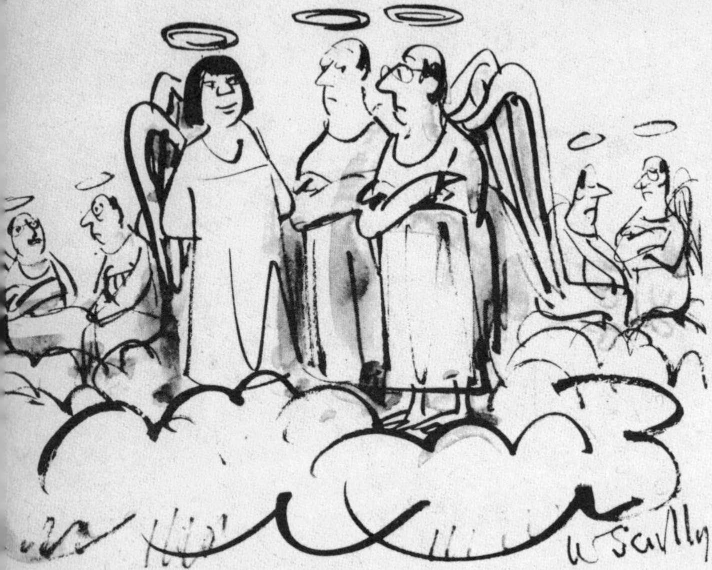

"I coveted all my neighbours' wives, but since I'm an Eskimo, apparently that was OK."

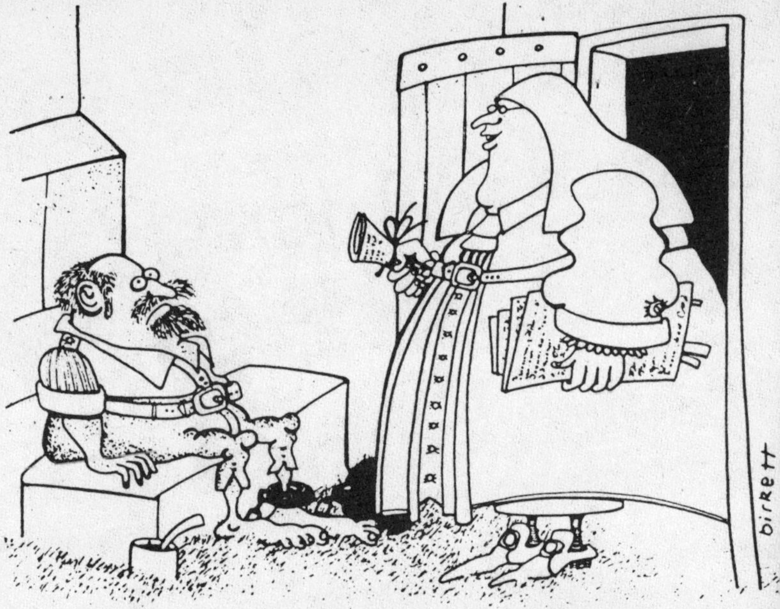

"The European Court has quashed your hanging, drawing and quartering sentence. You're to be hung, drawn and decimated."

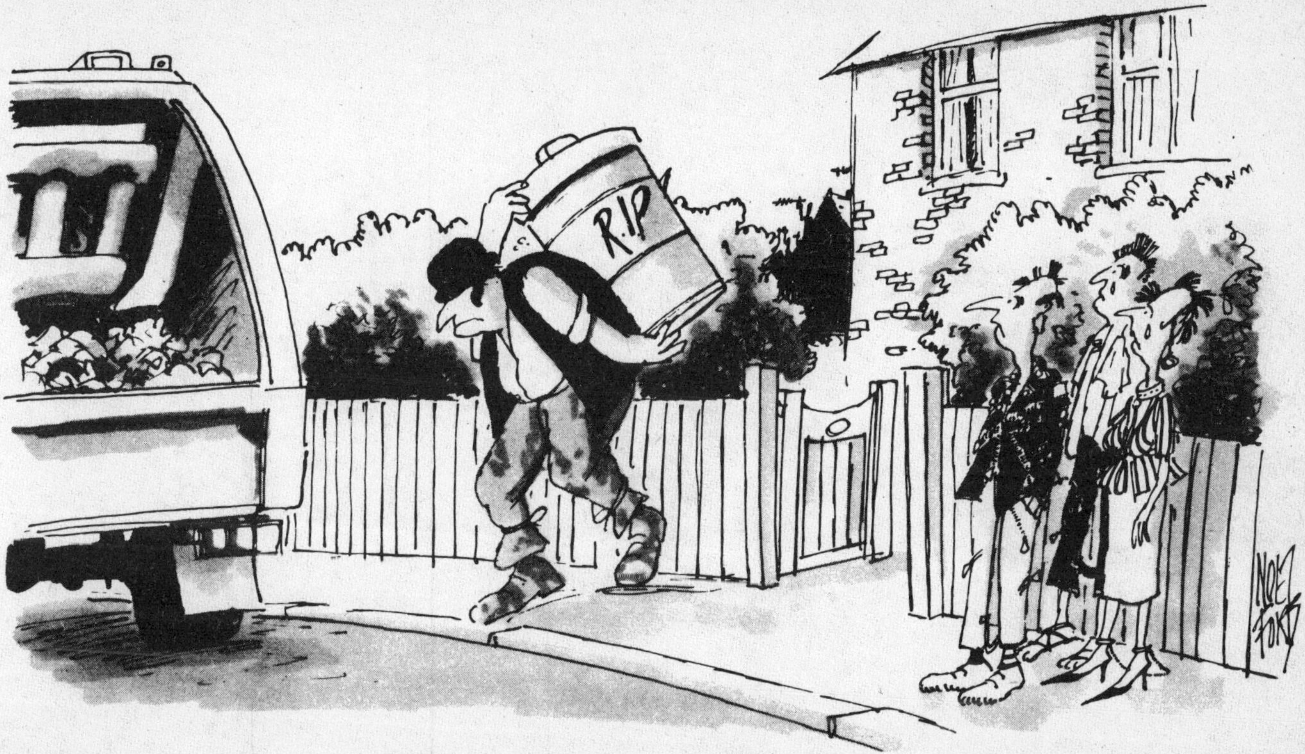
R.I.P
NOEL FORD

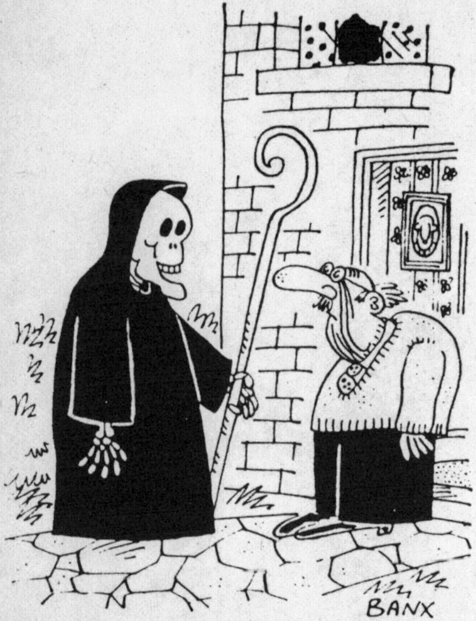

"It's a thankless job, but at least you get to meet people."

"He was a good boy who just got into a rotten crowd."

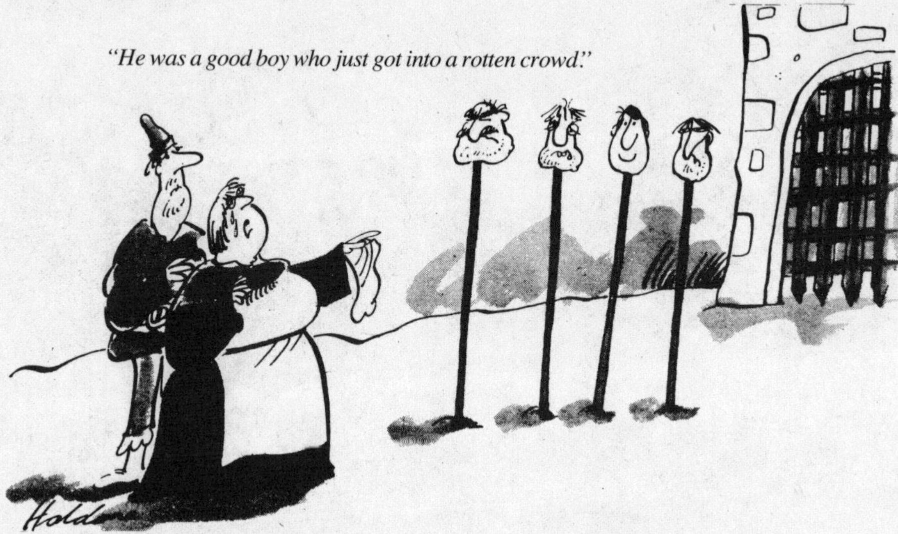

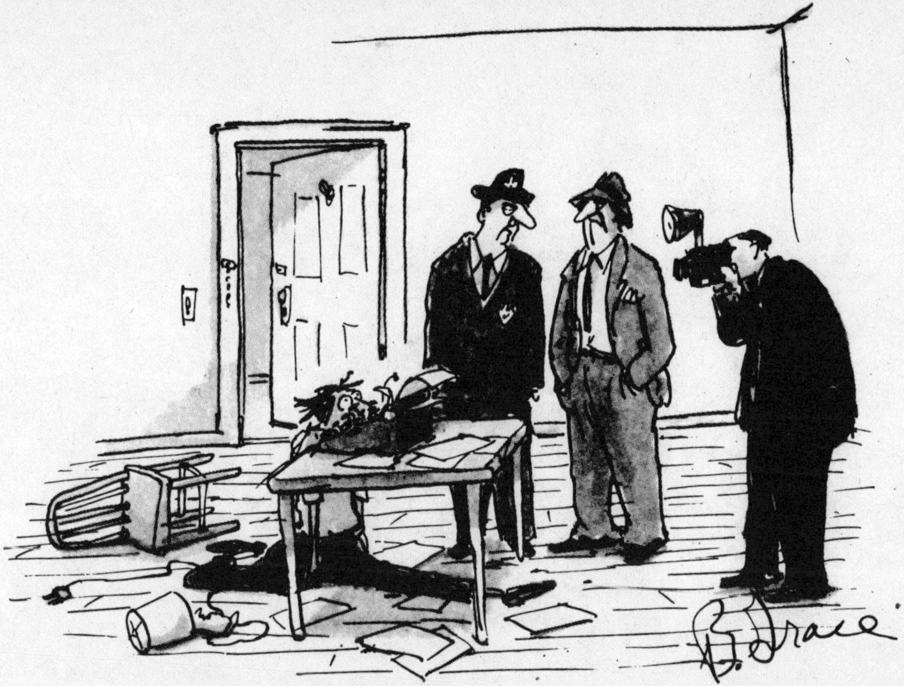

"We figure his nose got stuck in the keys, then he beat his brains out trying to type 'help'."

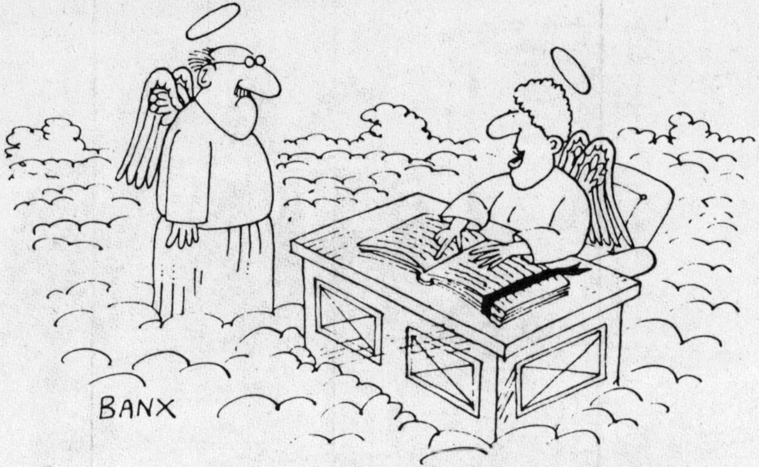

"You're being reincarnated as a mayfly, Mr Hoskins – have a nice day."

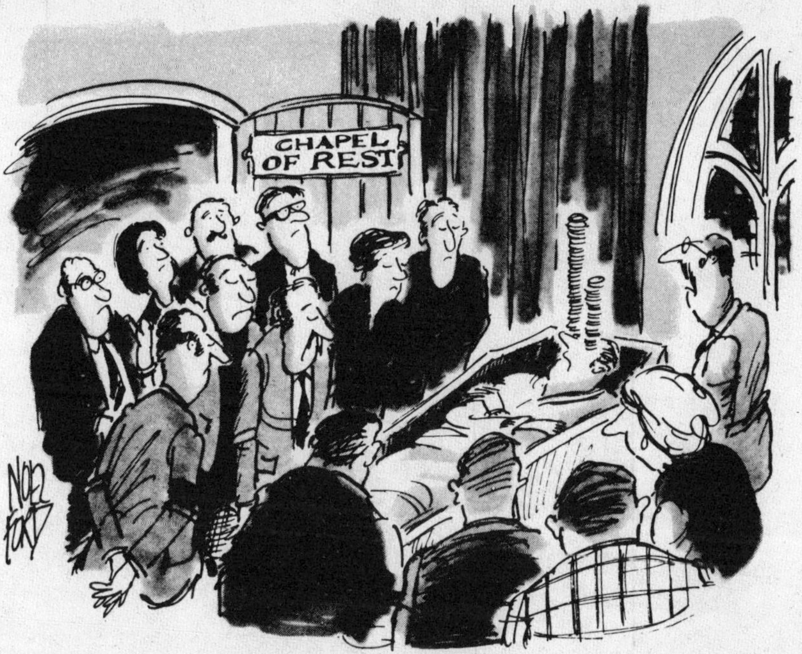

"He'll be sadly missed – as a charity fund-raiser at the Red Lion he was second to none."

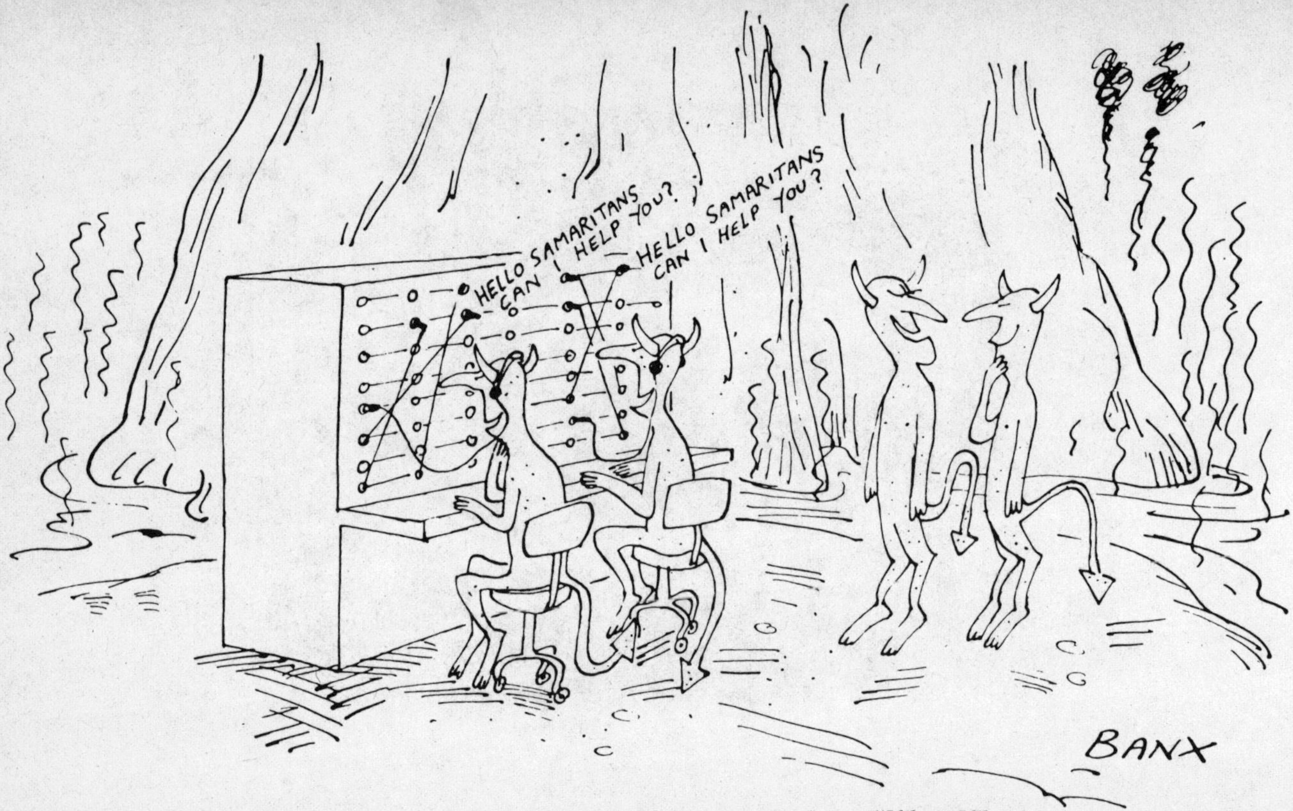

"I like it, I like it."

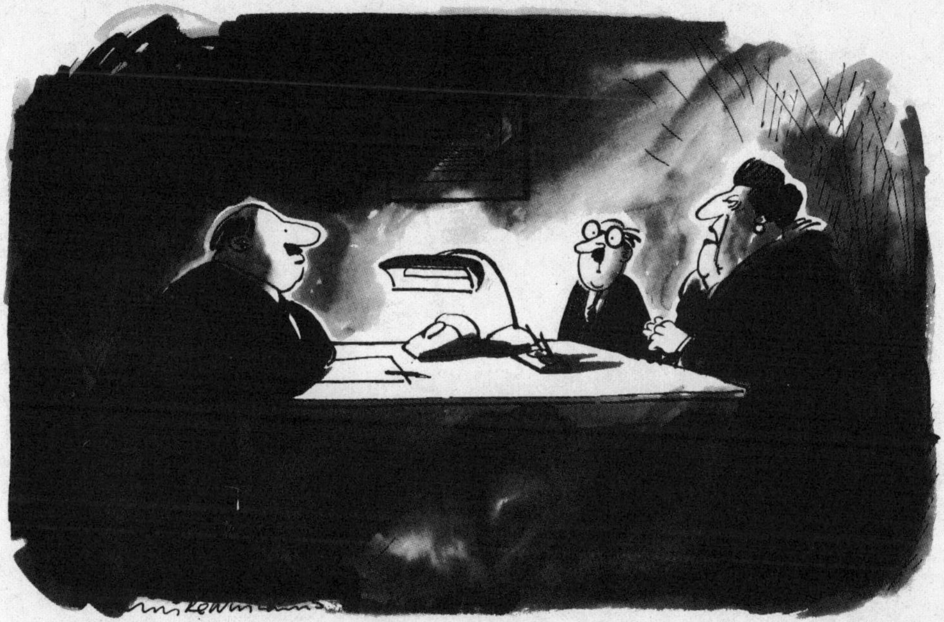

"I'm thinking of leaving his body to science."

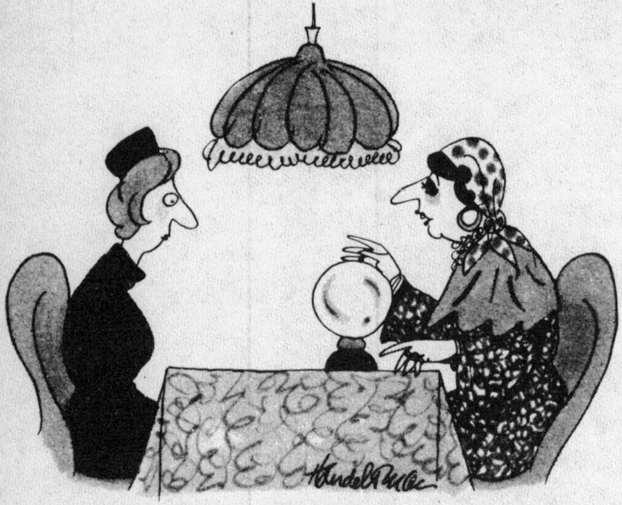

"Your late husband apologises for his long silence, and asks you to make allowances for his being dead."

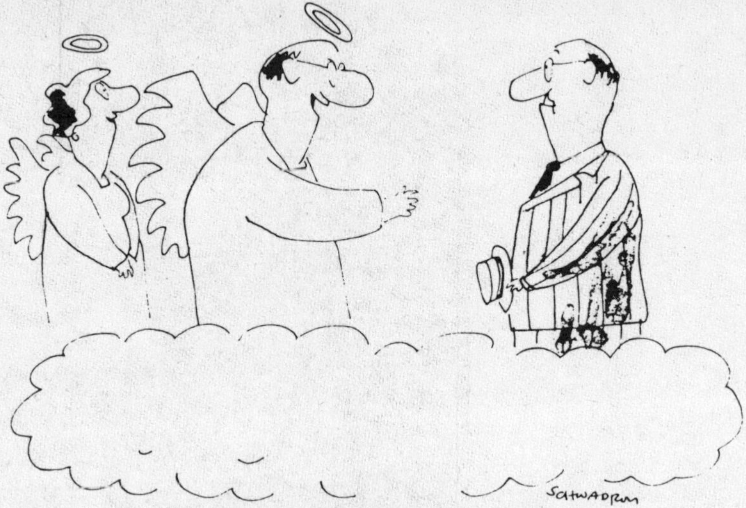

"Congratulations! What got you here is your total lack of commitment to any ideology."

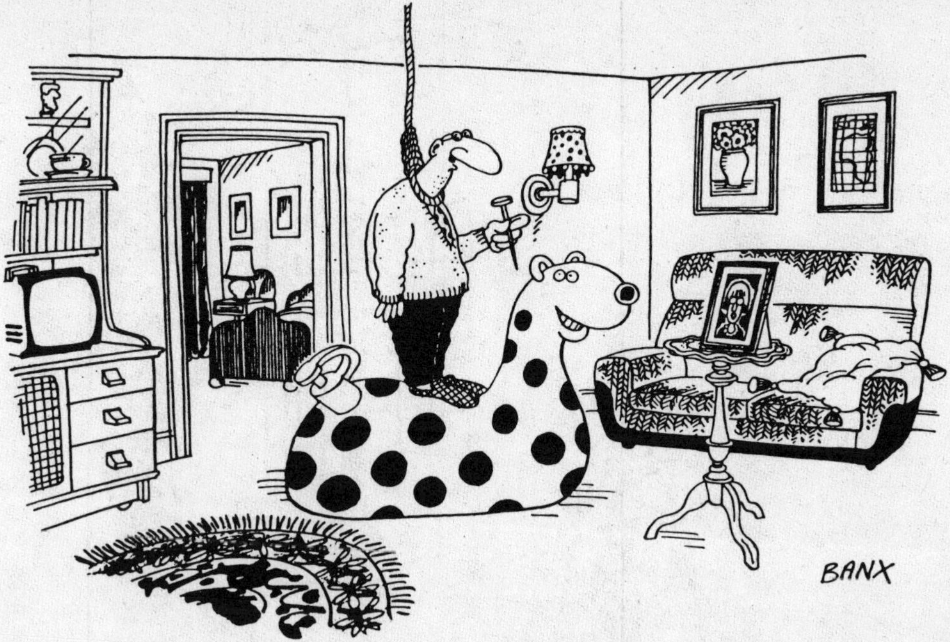
BANX

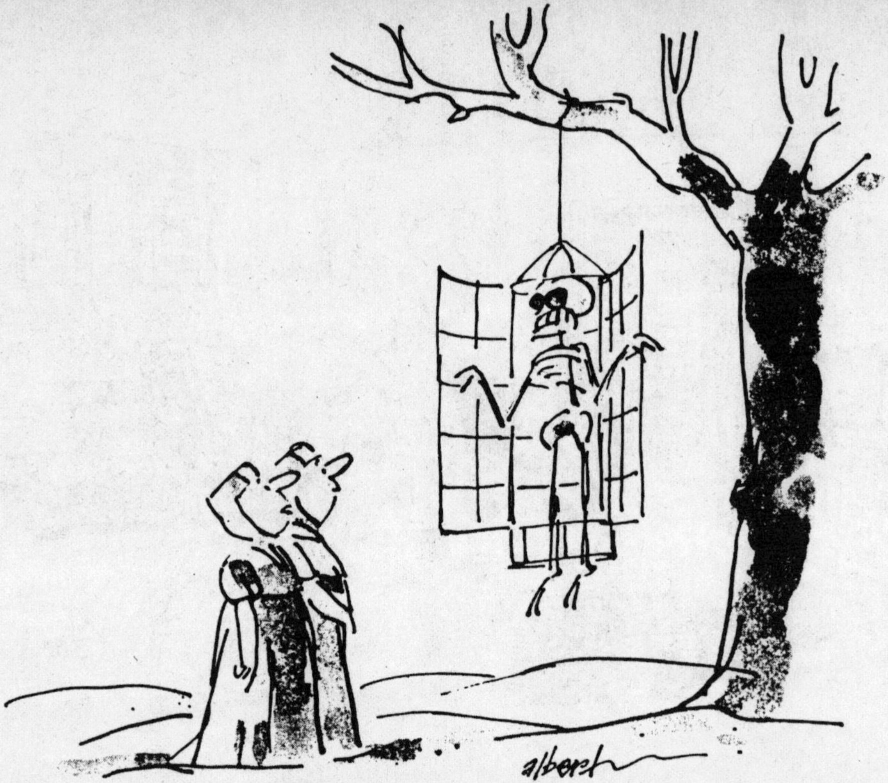

"Worst flasher Tyburn's ever seen."

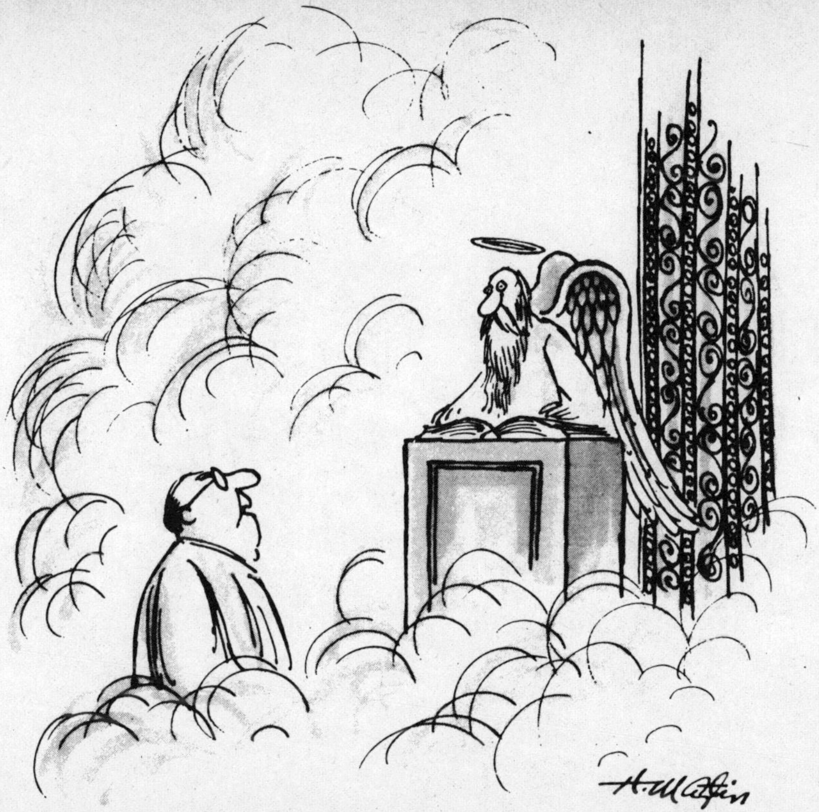

"I'm J. Harrison Follensby. Which way to the executive washroom?"

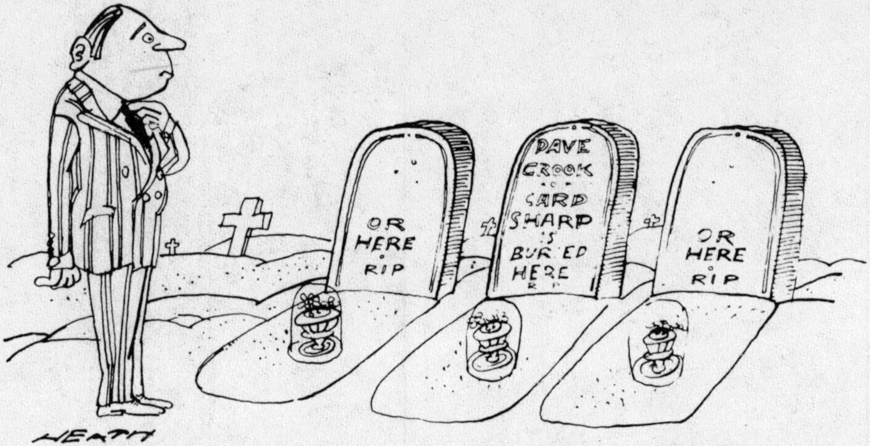
OR HERE RIP
DAVE CROOK CARD SHARP IS BURIED HERE
OR HERE RIP
HEATH

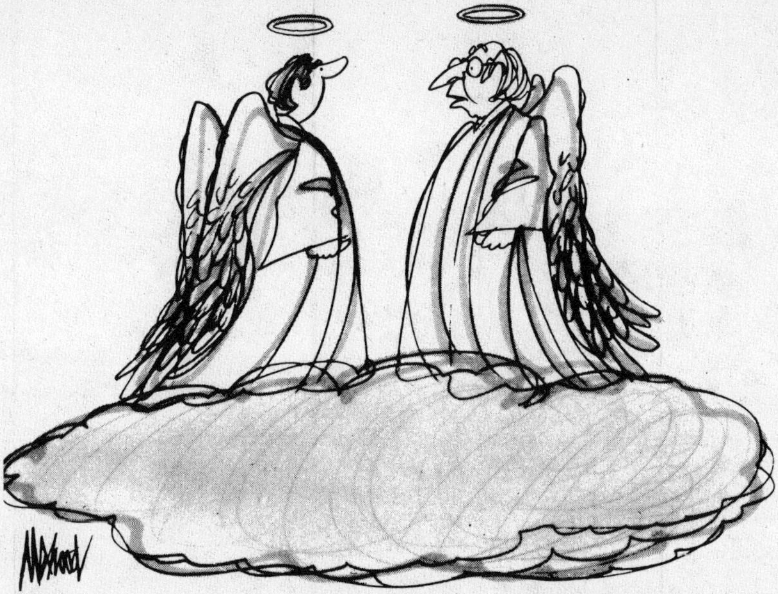

"If it hadn't been for all that damn health food, I could have been up here years ago."

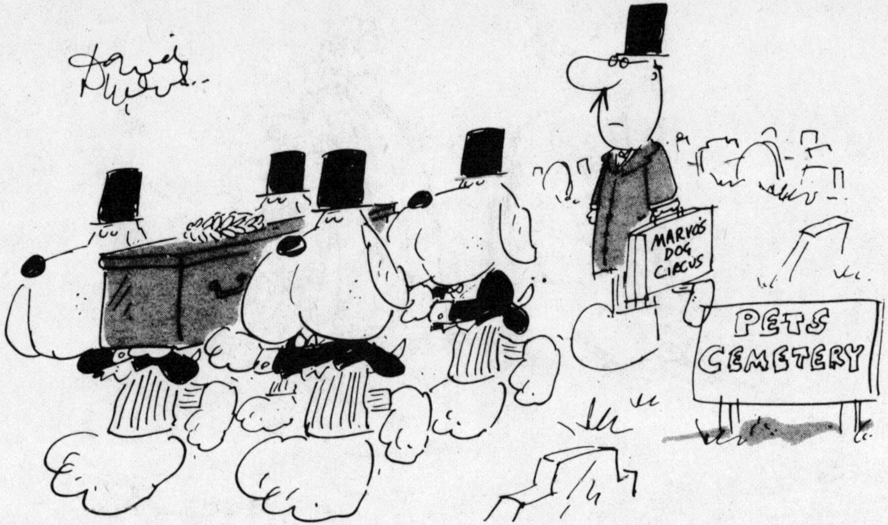
MARVO'S DOG CIRCUS
PETS CEMETERY

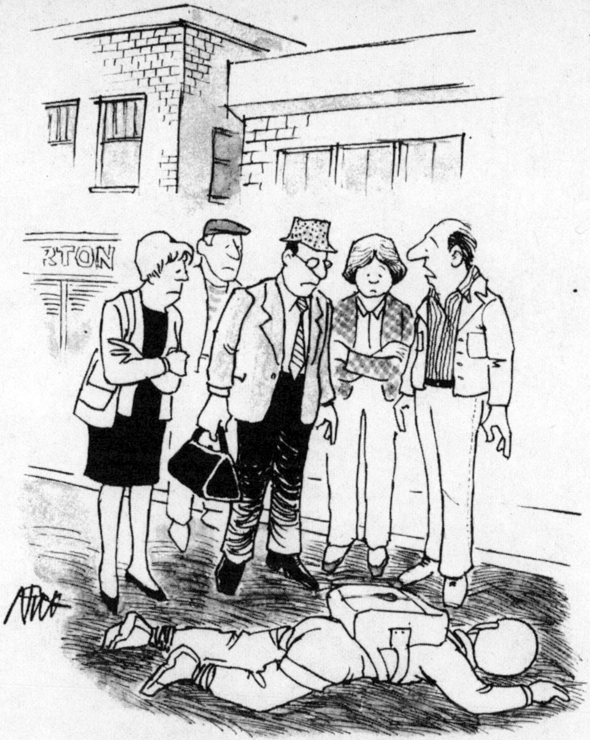

"Don't know how much good it'll do, but
I loosened his parachute."

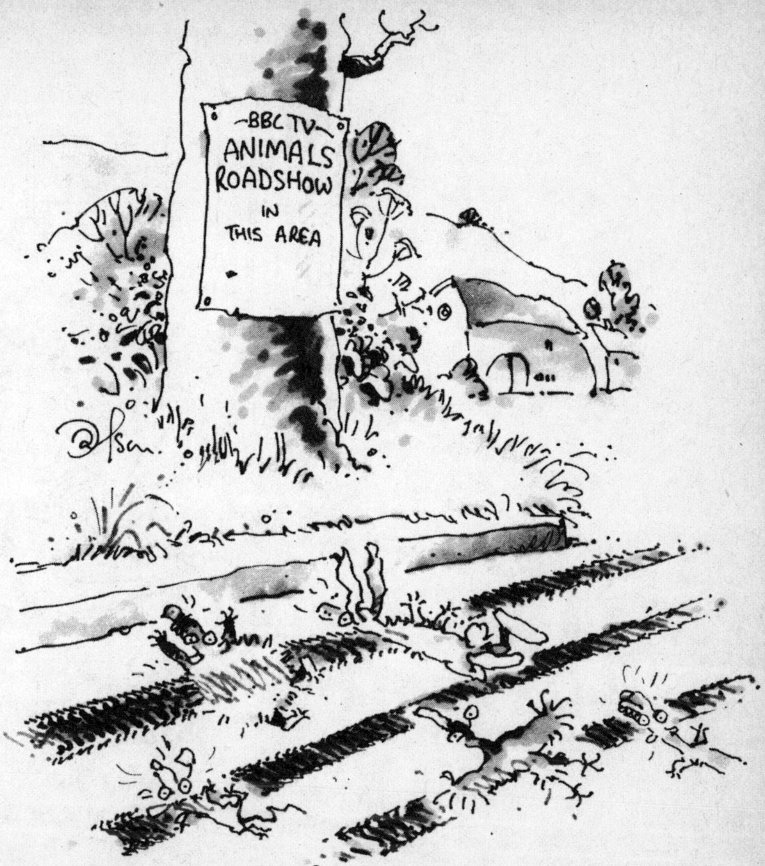

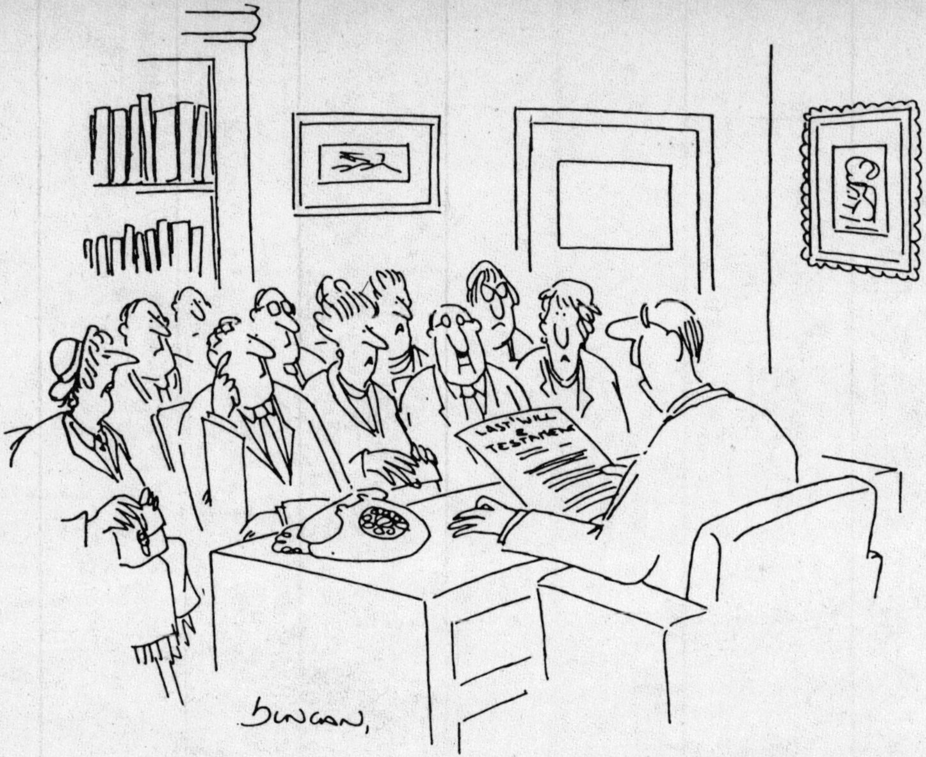

"And to the rest of you who were unlucky this time, I leave my thanks for attending, my condolences, and the sincere belief that you will try again."

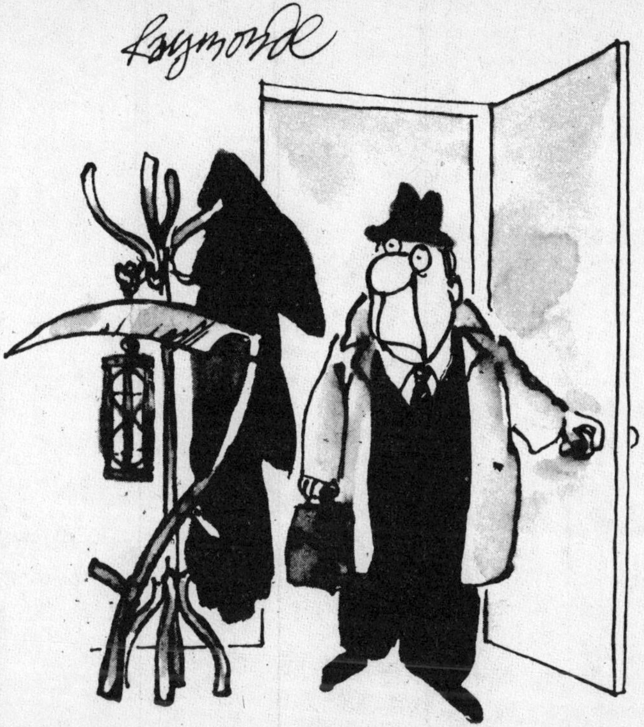

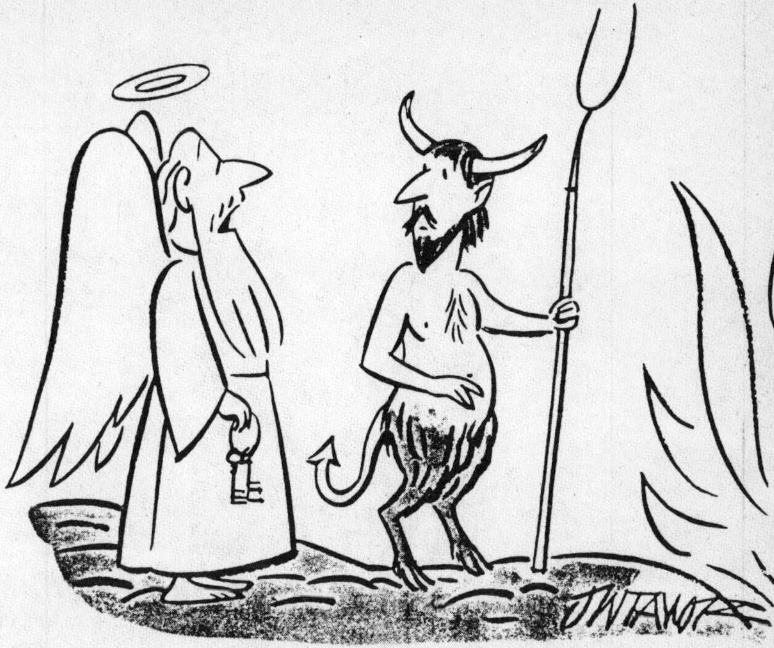

"I thought perhaps we ought to have a co-ordinated crowd control plan in case deterrence doesn't work."

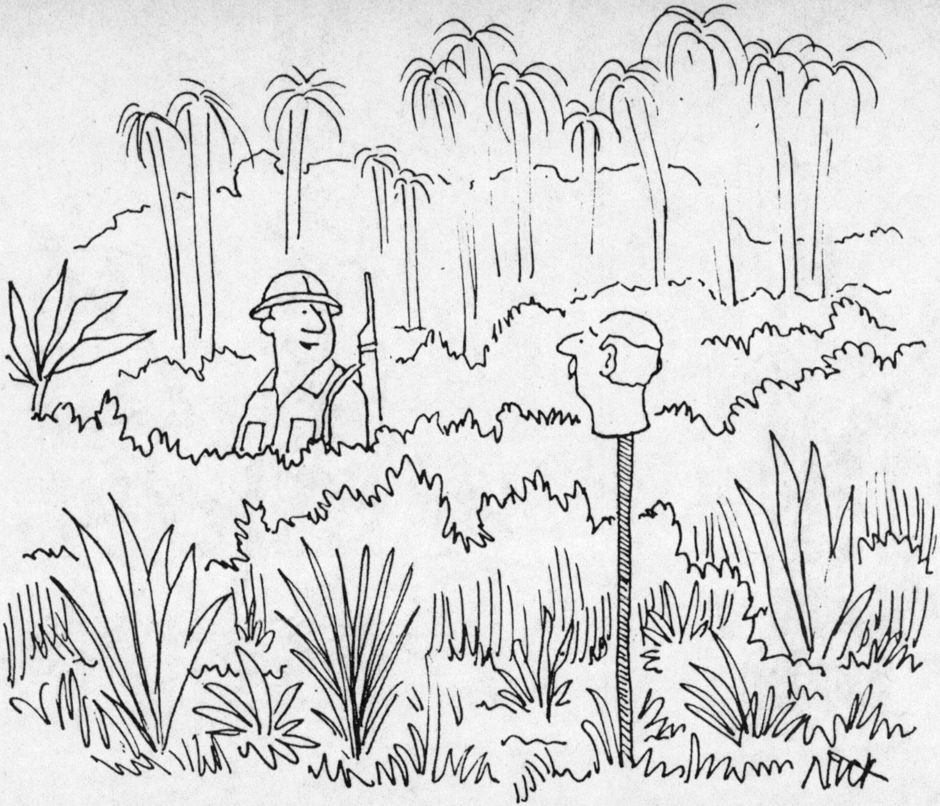

"Ah, there you are, Protheroe. I was beginning to think the fuzzie-wuzzies had got you."

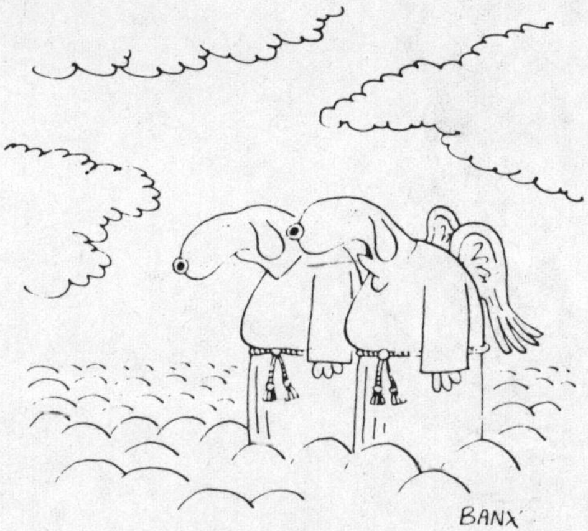

"I was rather hoping there'd be smoking after death."

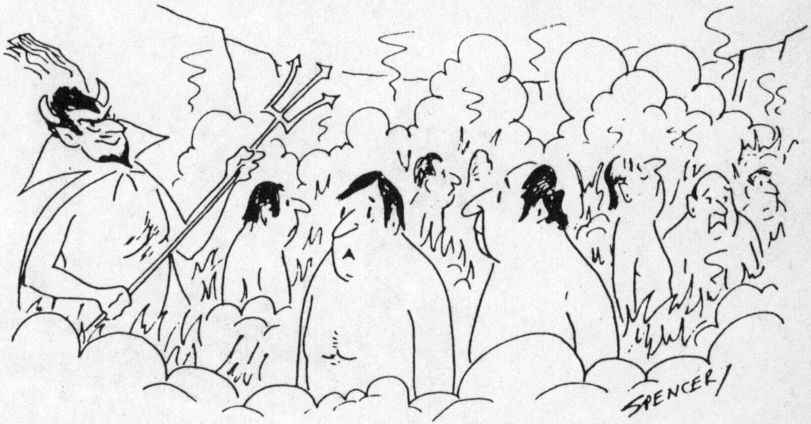

*"Sid Parker's wife certainly wasn't worth **this**!"*

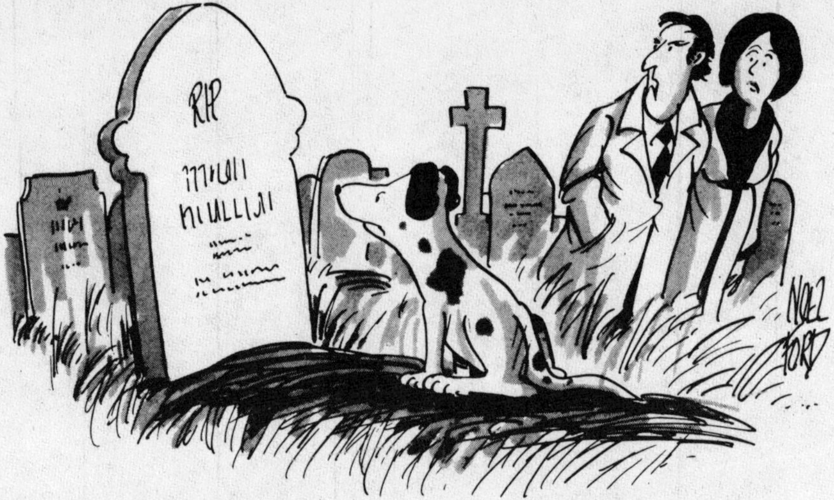

"Touching, be damned – it was a condition of the will."

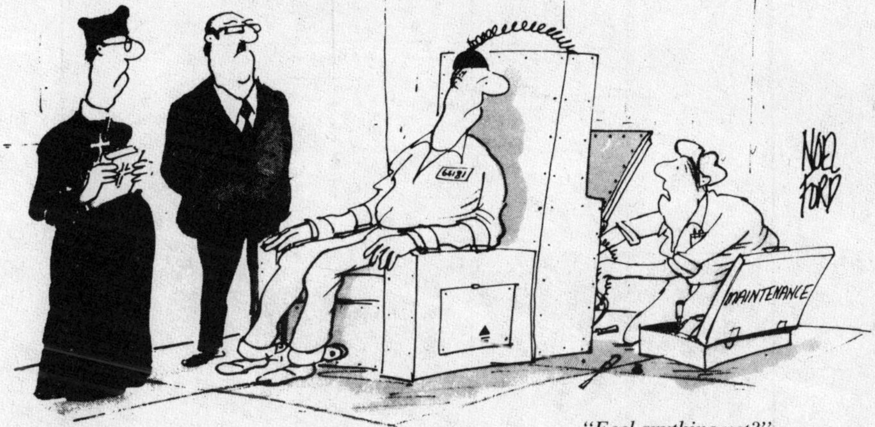

"Feel anything yet?"

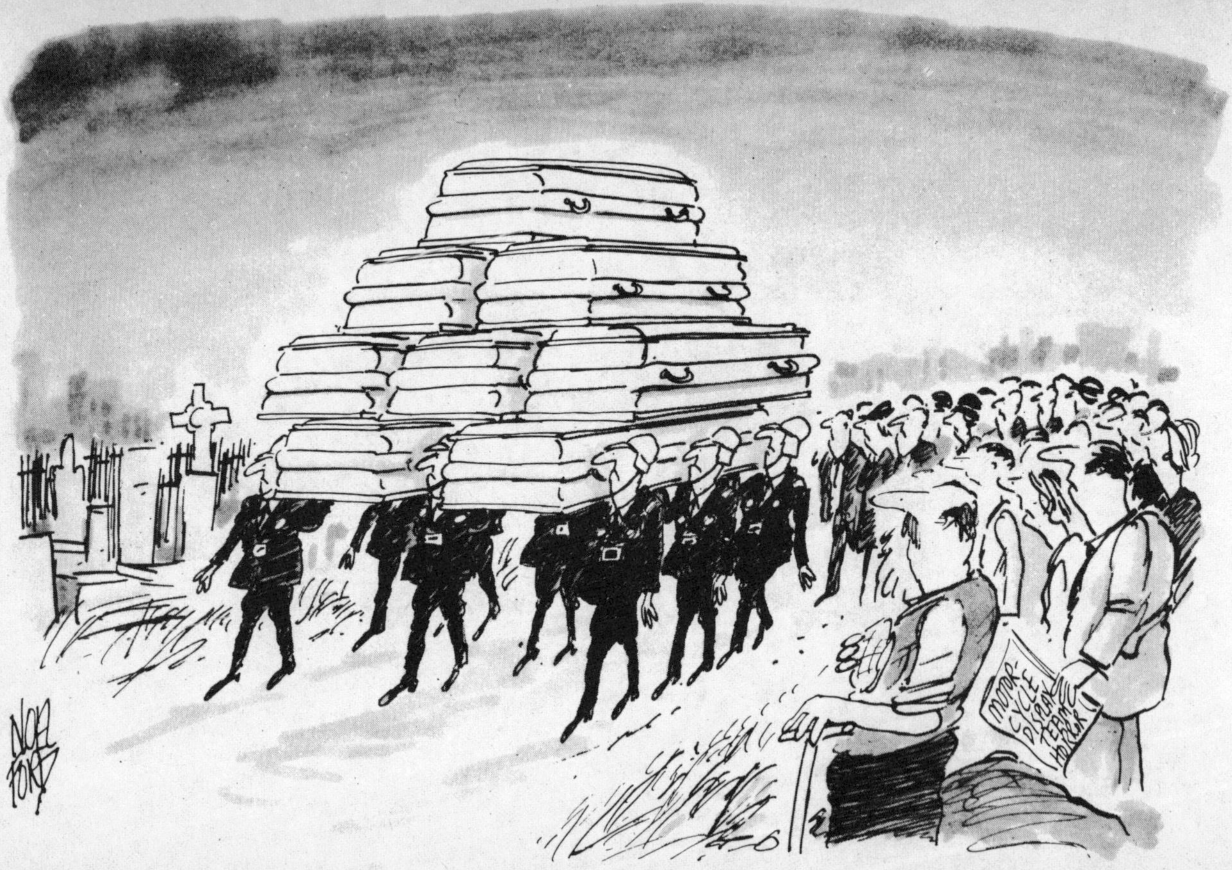
NOEL FORD
MOTOR-CYCLE DISPLAY TEAM HORROR

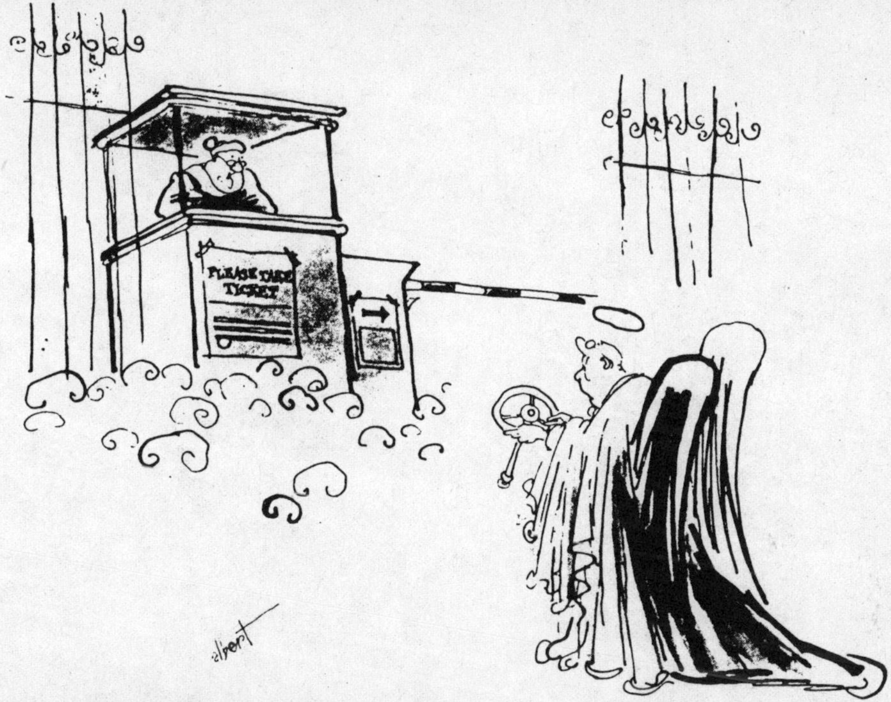

"National Car Parks took it over years ago!"

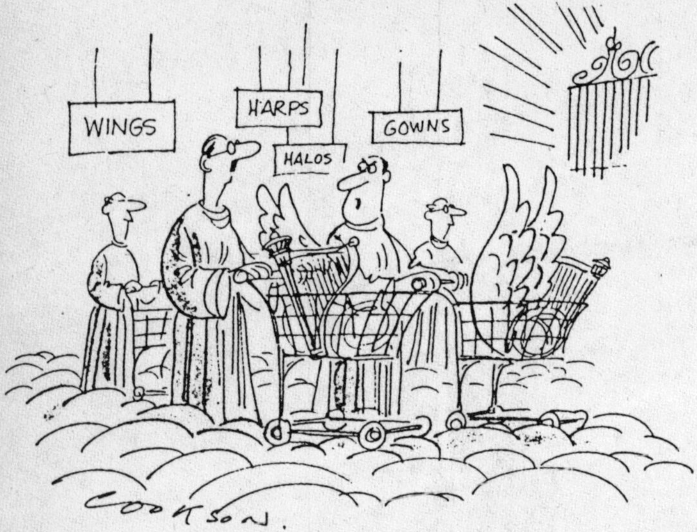

"I don't care how it looks, this has got to be hell!"

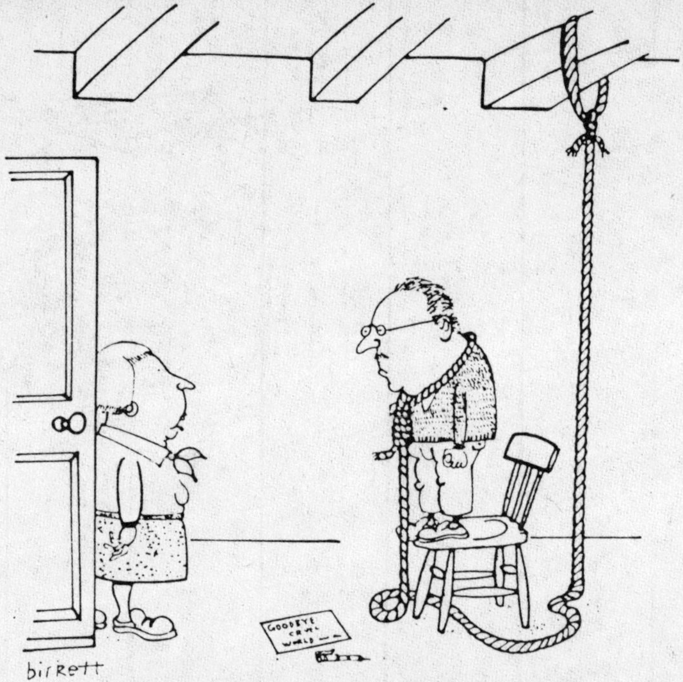

"Oh, Gerald – you haven't failed the entrance test for Mensa again?"

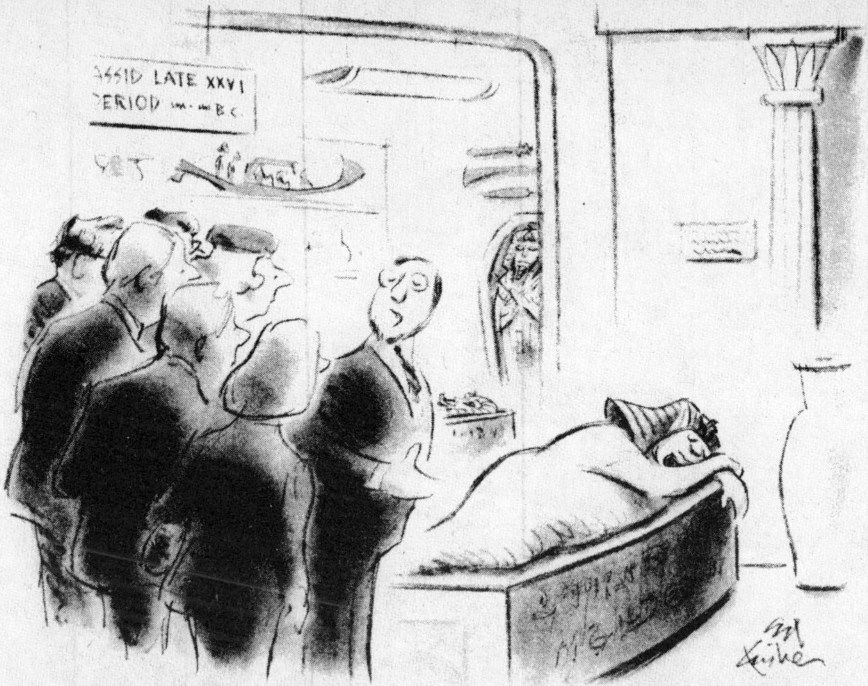

"The funerary art of ***this*** *dynasty is considerably less formal than its predecessors'."*

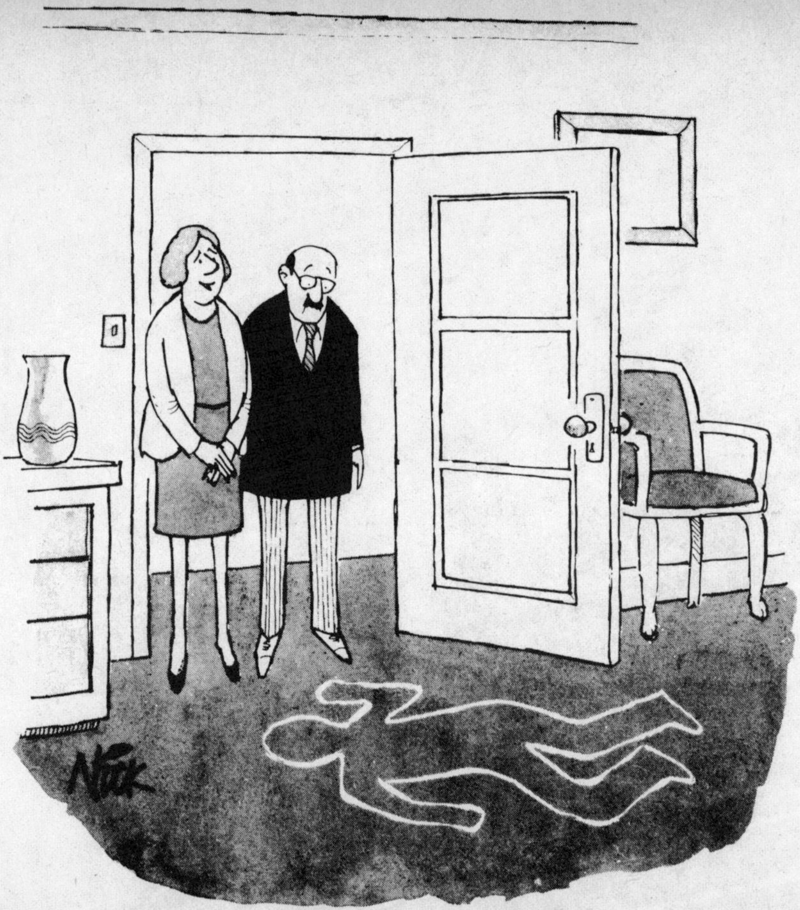

"I've kept poor George's room exactly as it was the day he died."

"Of all his showbiz friends,
you had to invite that flamin' Emu!"

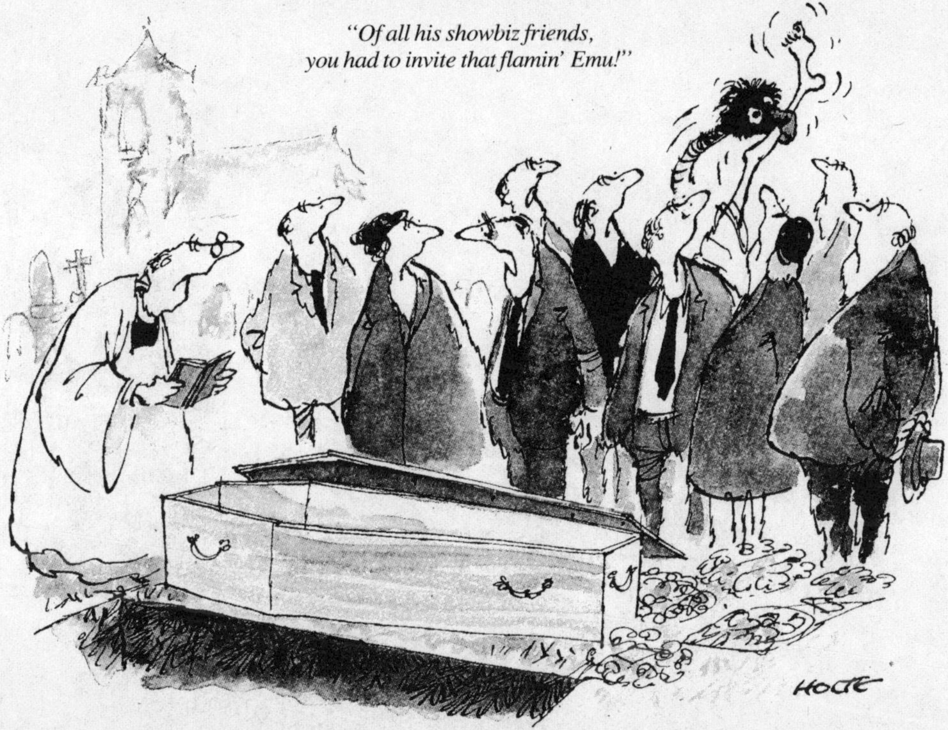

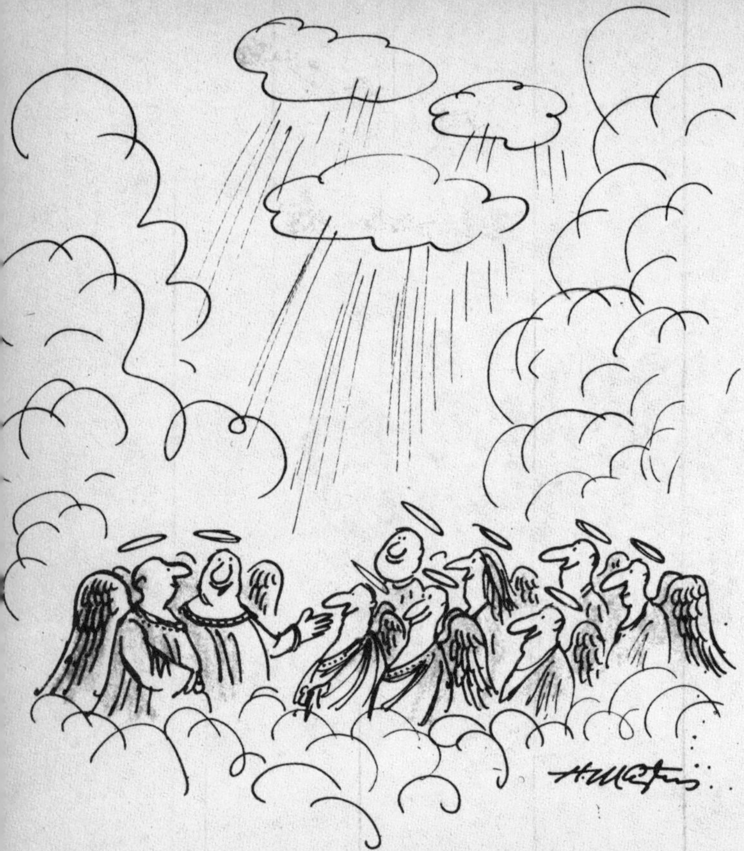

"Alfred The Great, you remember Peter The Great, Ferdinand The Great, Catherine The Great, Charles The Great and Frederick The Great, don't you?"

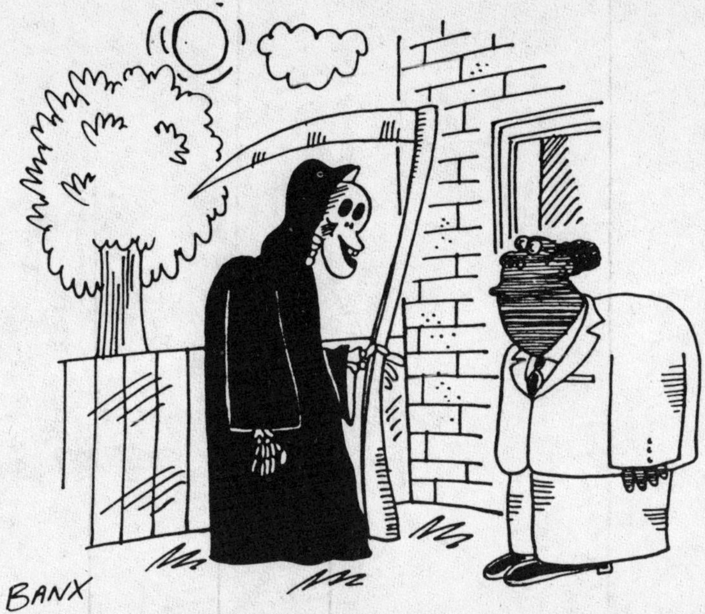

"Not many people realise I was black myself once, Mr Frinton."

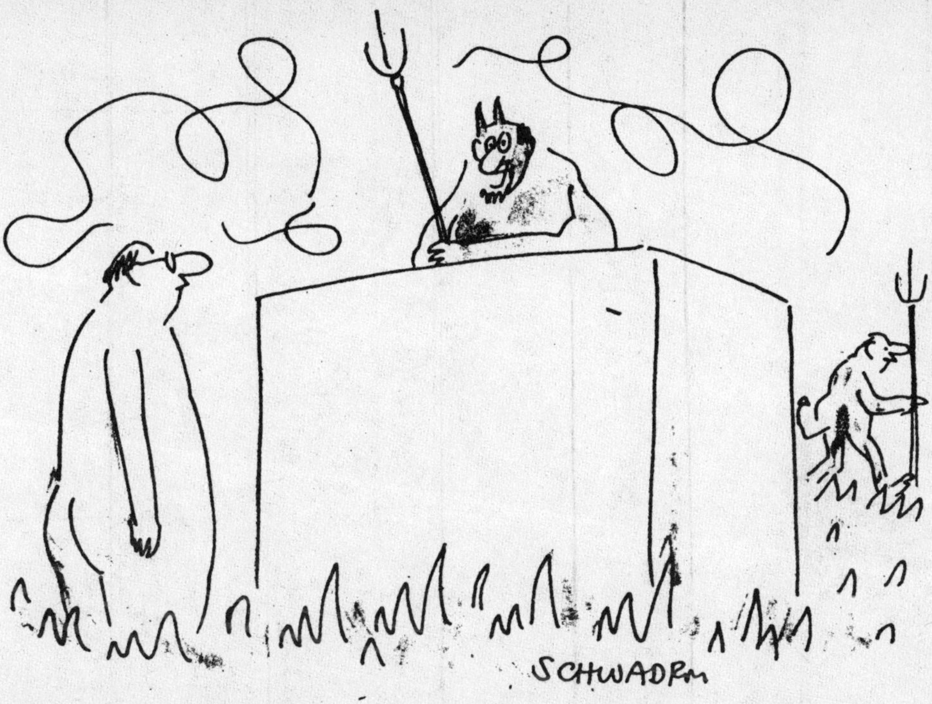

"Hi, my name is Lennie and I'll be your persecutor down here."

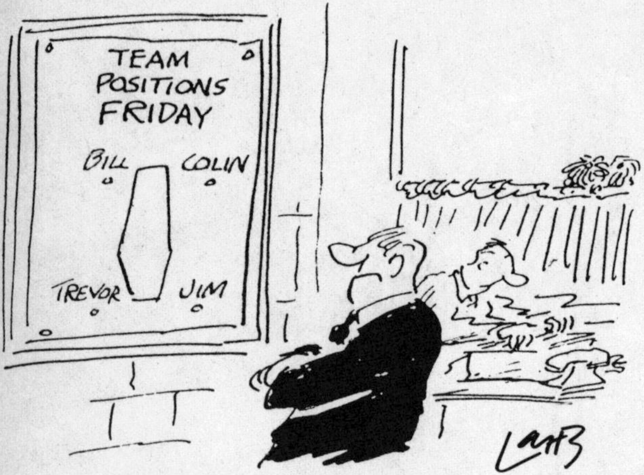

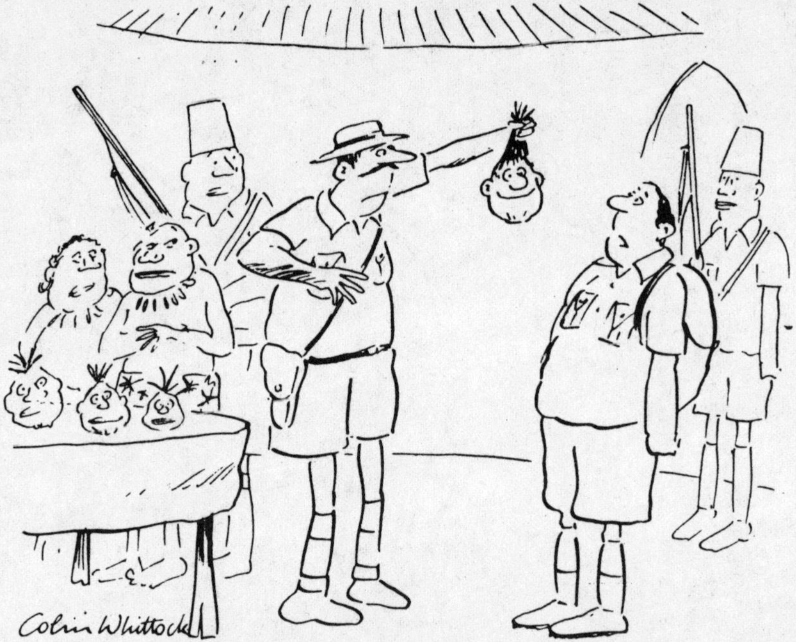

"No, that isn't my brother – he wasn't that tall . . ."

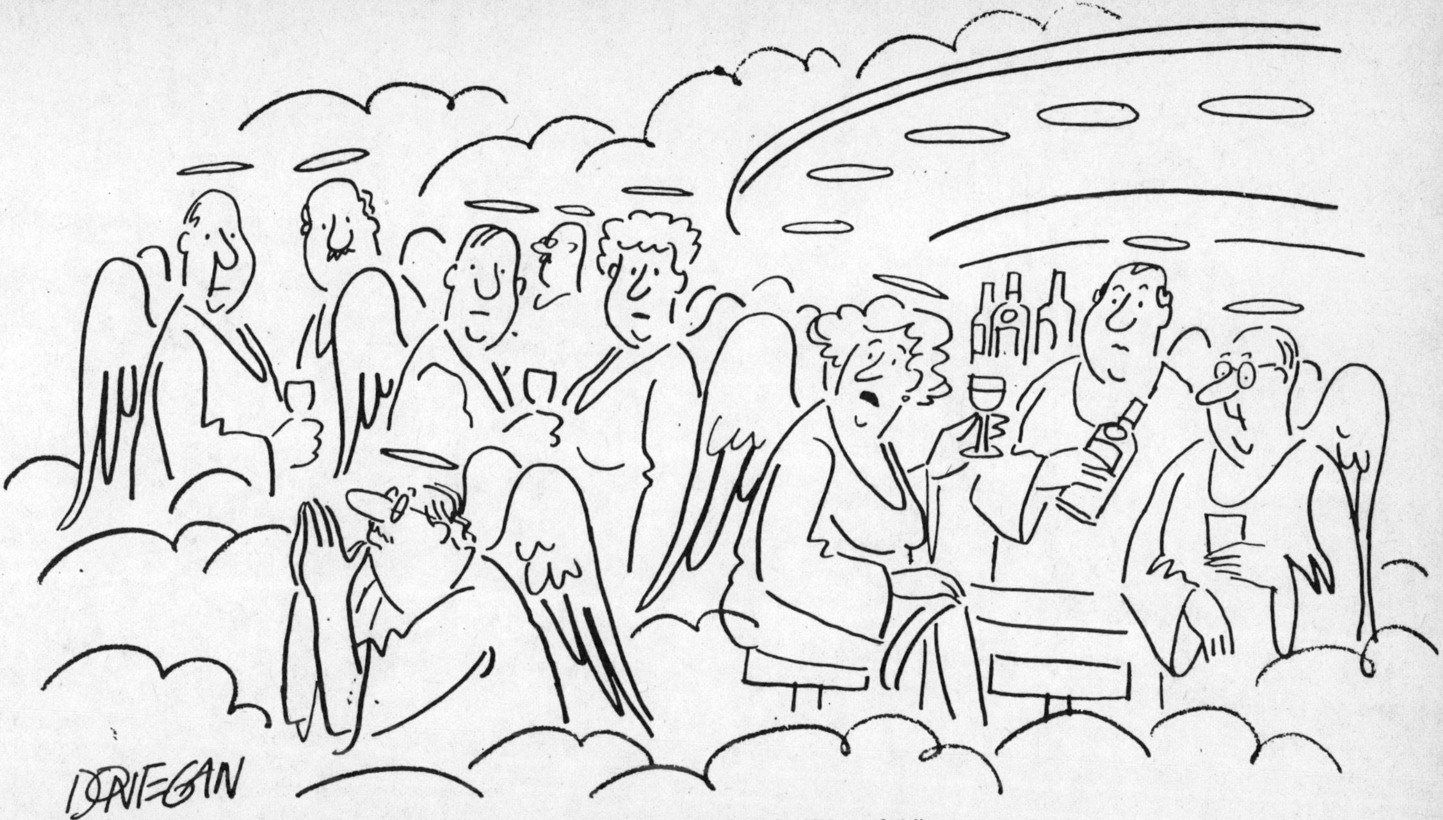

"For pity's sake, Norman, relax! We made it."

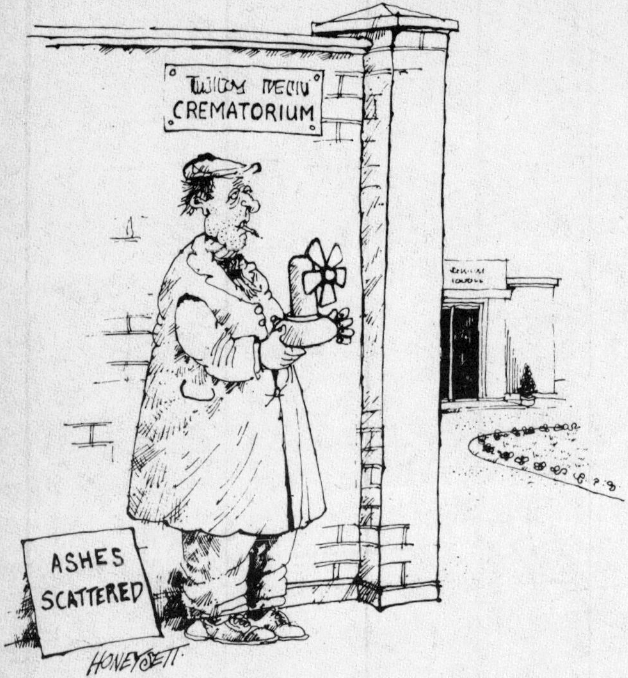

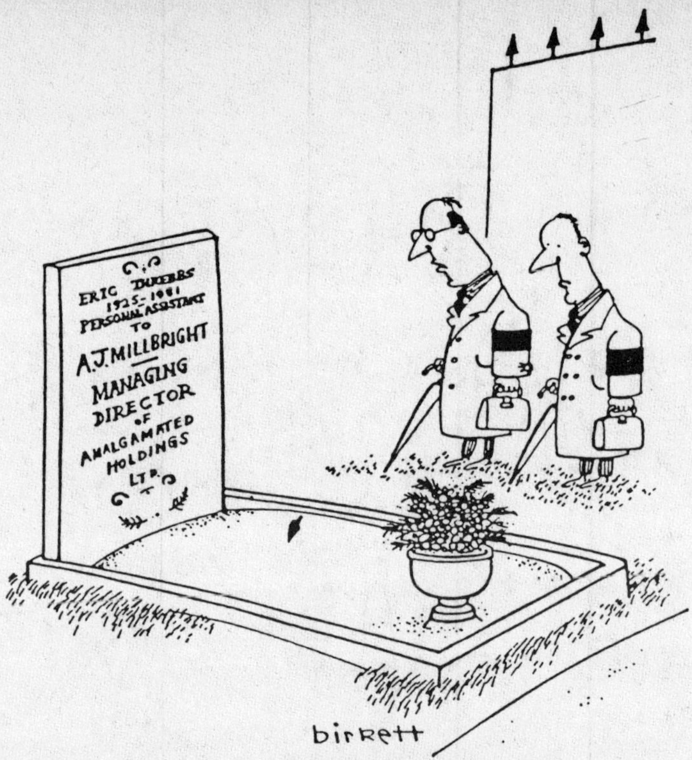

"I told you he'd be missed – I can hear his pocket bleeper going."

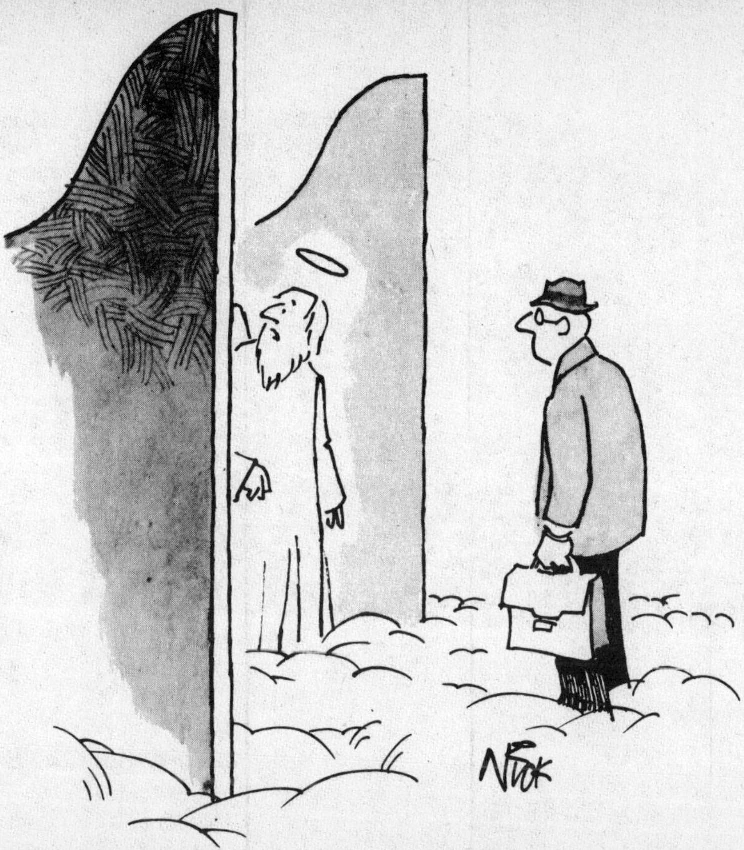

"Anyone here interested in the Jehovah's Witnesses?"

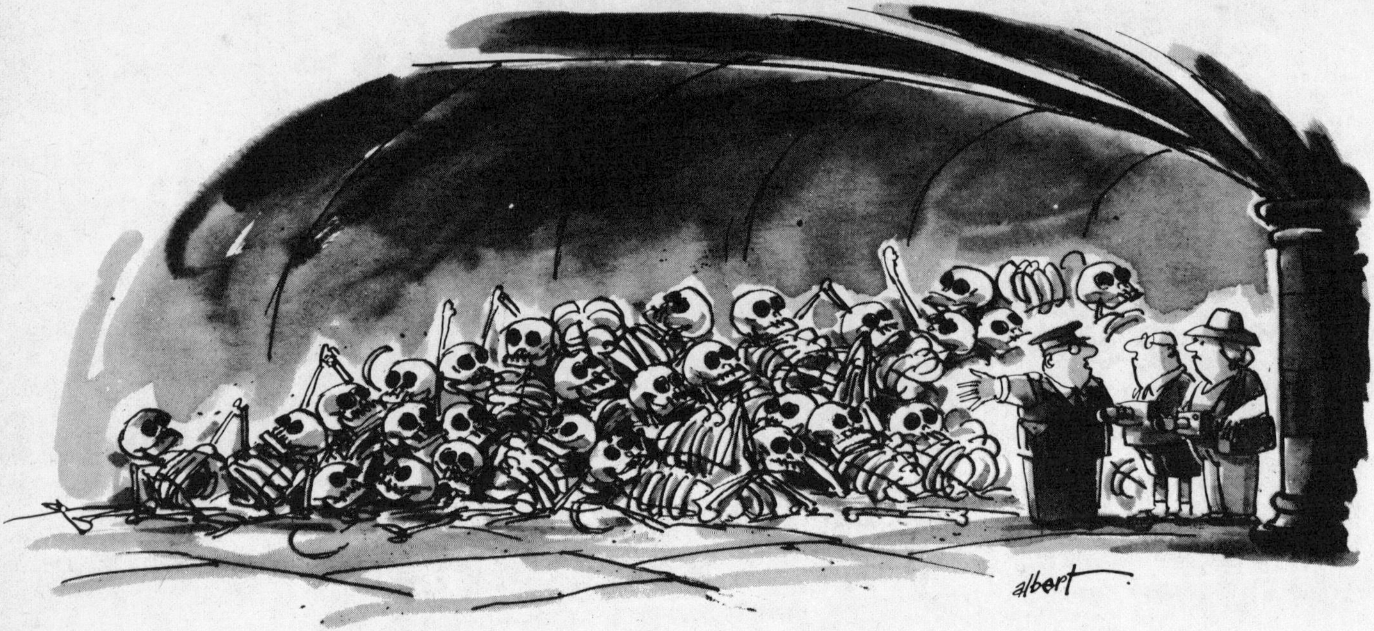

"Trips around the catacombs, sir. Back of the queue!"

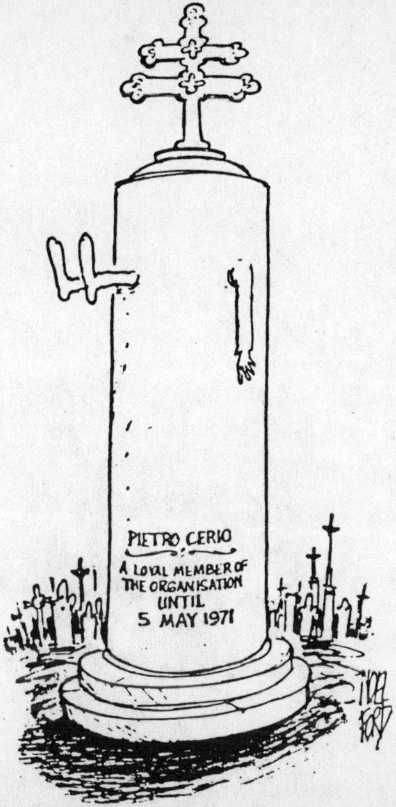

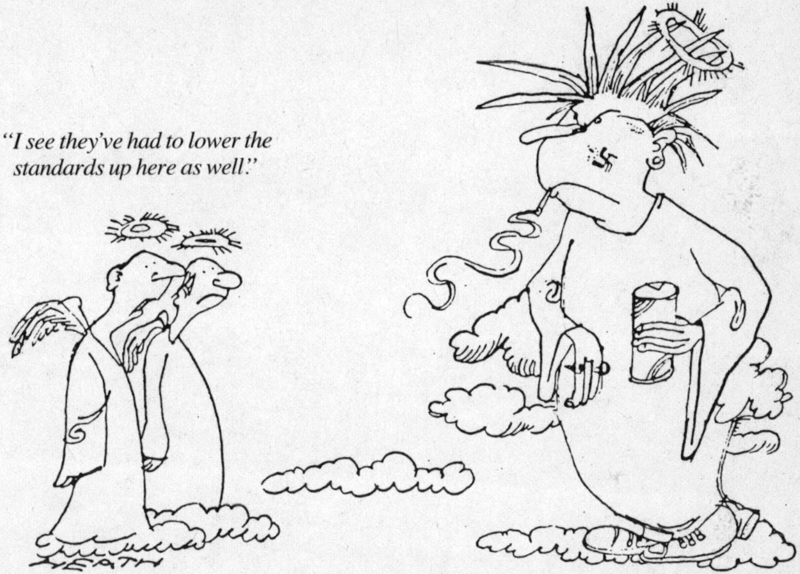

"I see they've had to lower the standards up here as well."

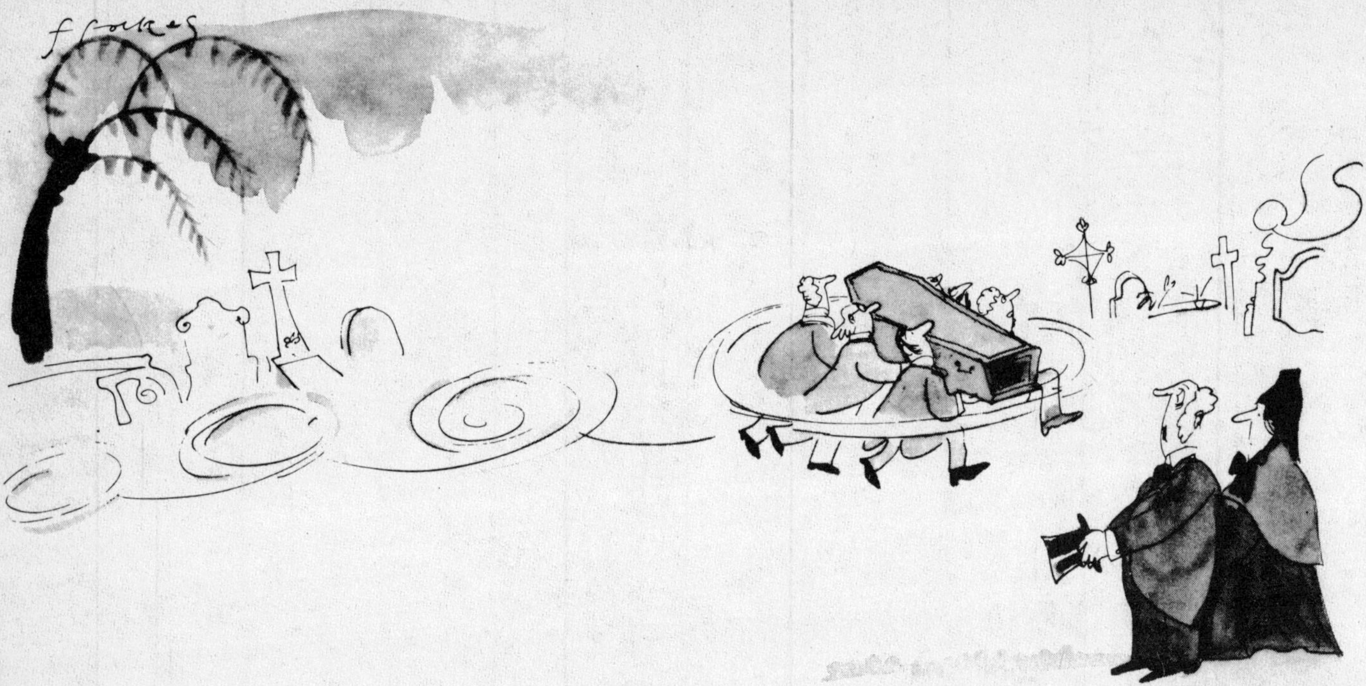

"I know they intend it as a compliment but I think they should show more respect for Johann."

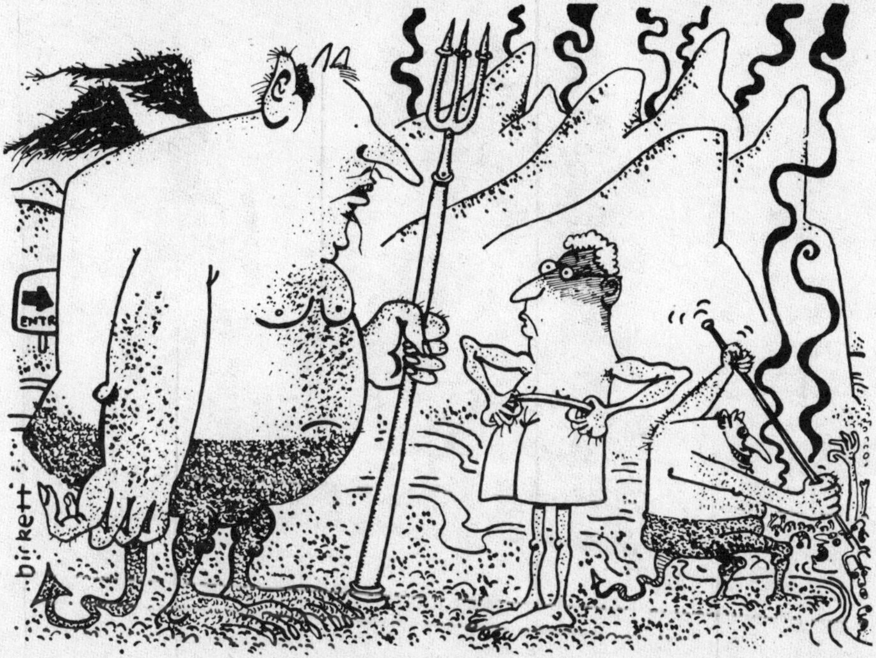

*"No, I'm sorry – if **I** let **you** keep your underpants on, I'd have to let **everyone** keep their underpants on."*

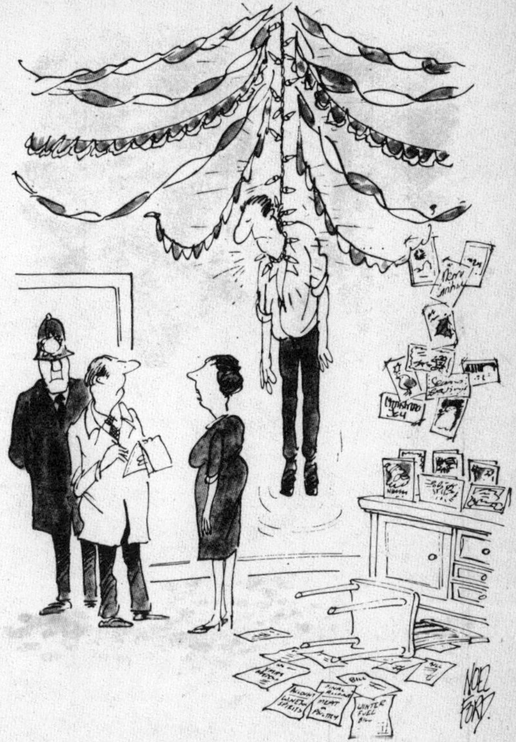

"Of course, I shan't be cutting him down before Twelfth Night."

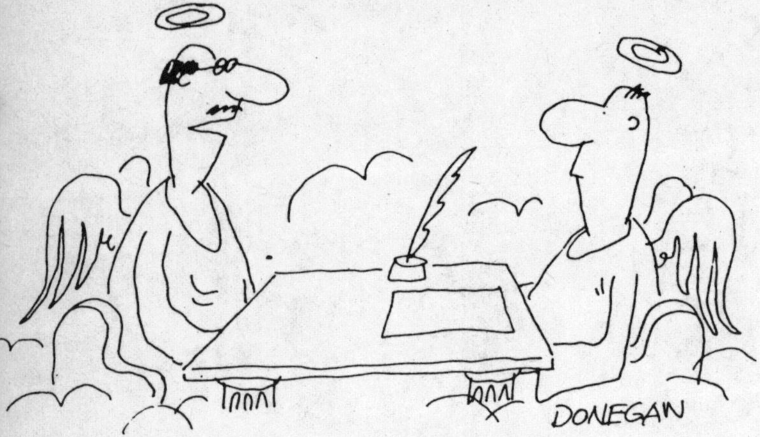

"I think it's time I started putting something by for my Resurrection."

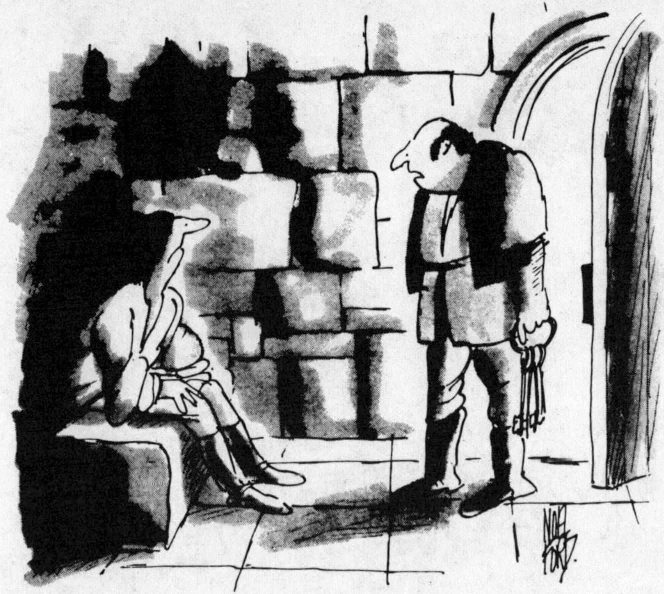

"Oh, come on, you can think of a better last request than an early morning call."

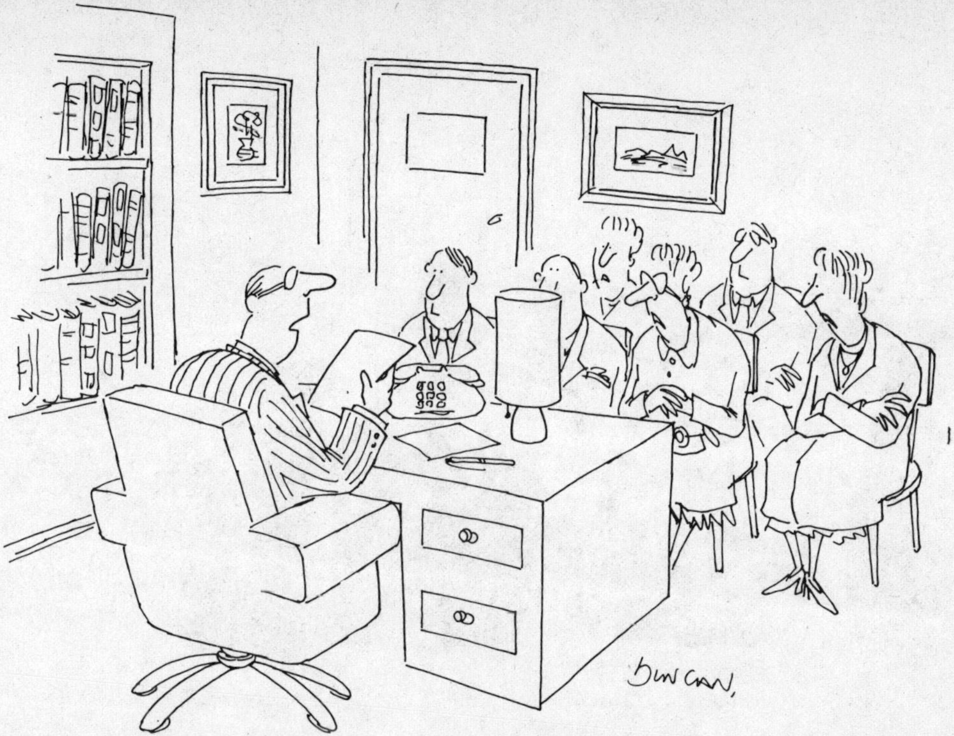

"To my second wife, Joan, I leave the news of our bigamous marriage."

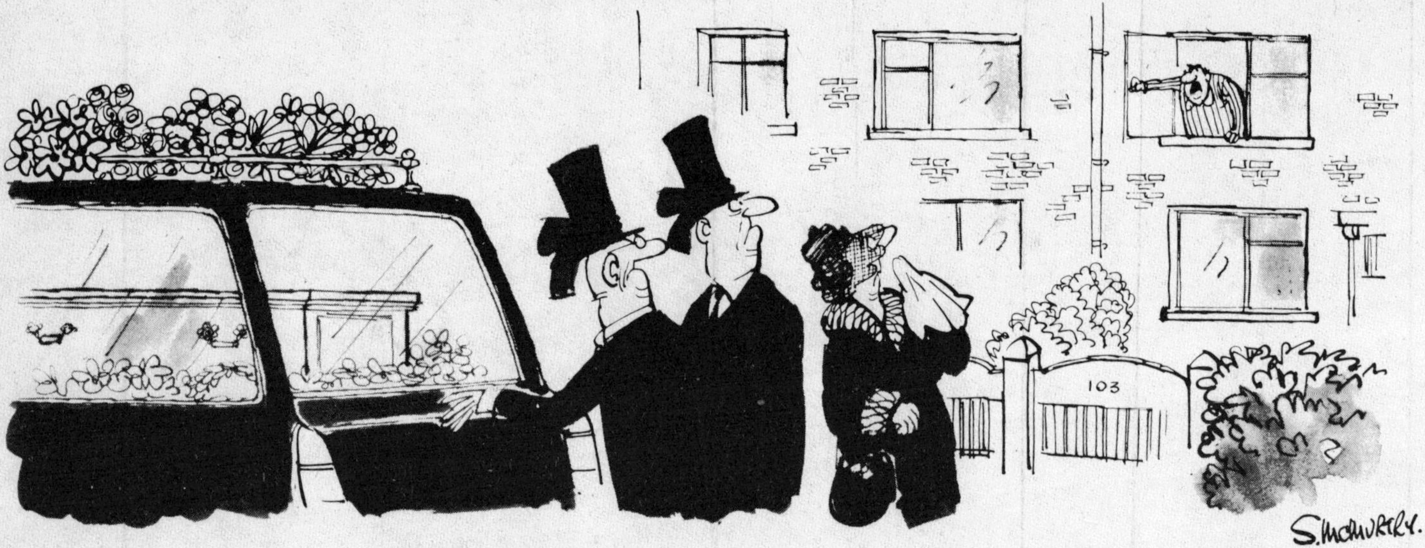

"Have you no consideration? Last week it was ambulances tearing up and down, slamming doors!"

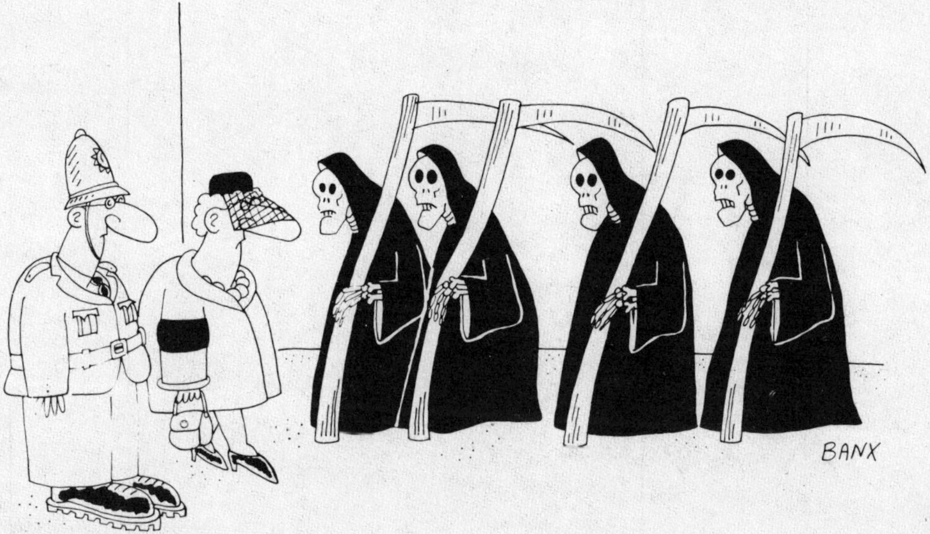
BANX

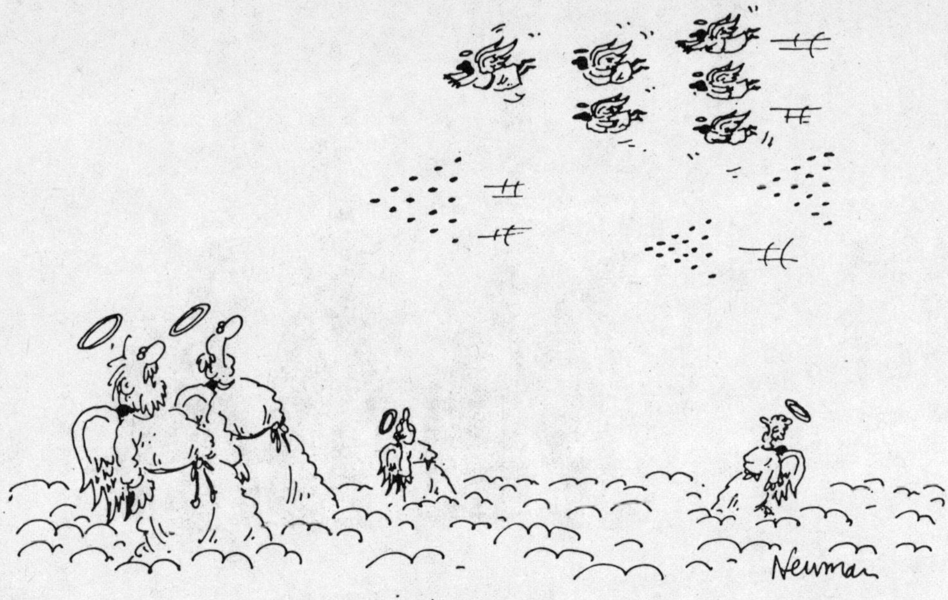

"The Africans always migrate south for the winter."

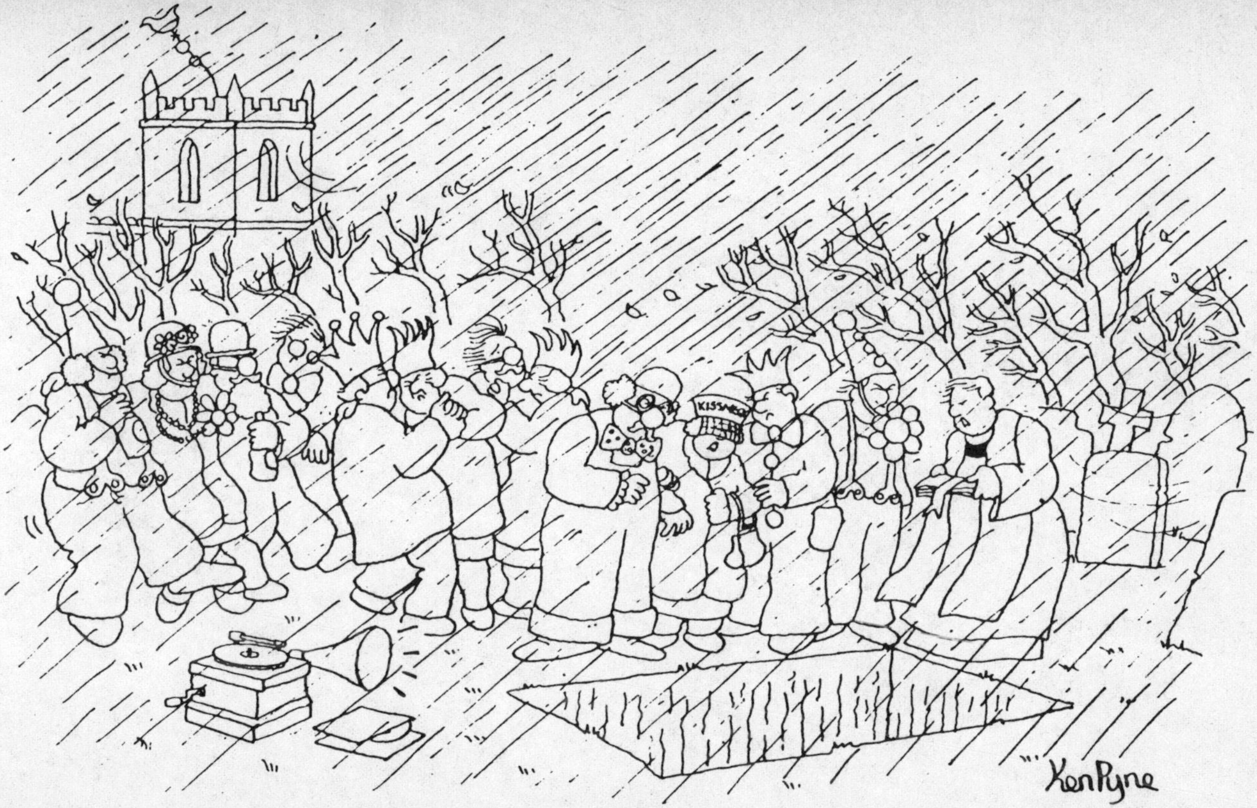

"It was a condition of his will – he didn't want anyone to be miserable at his funeral."

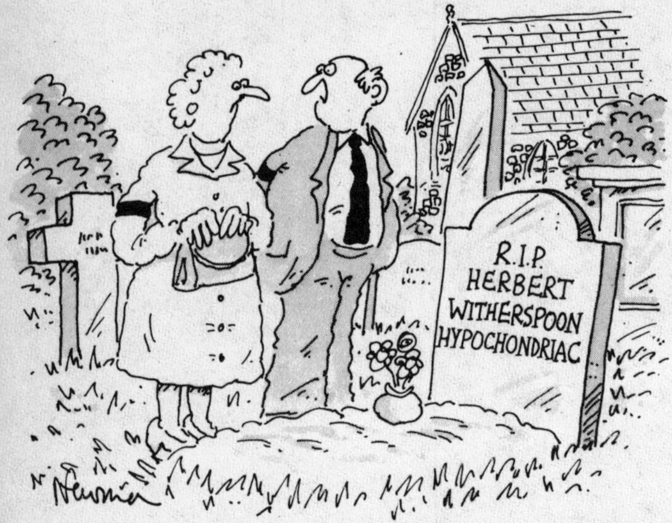

"He's not really dead, you know."

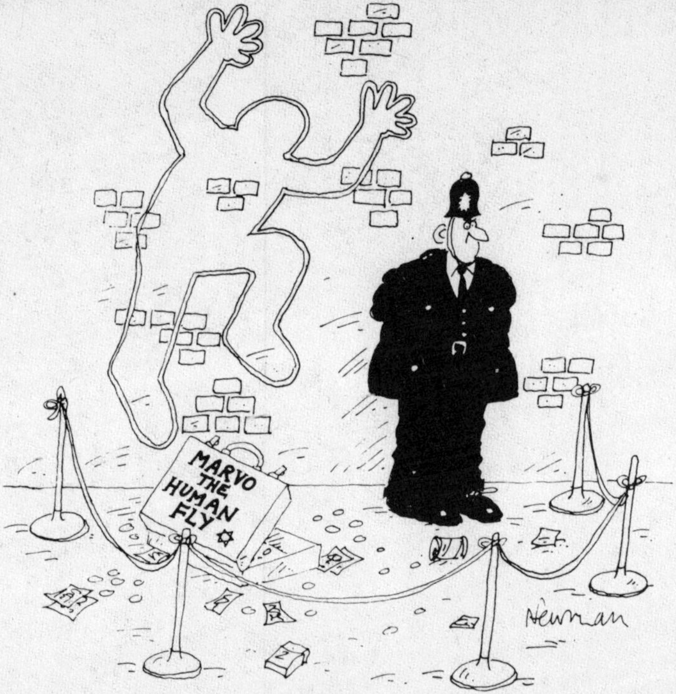

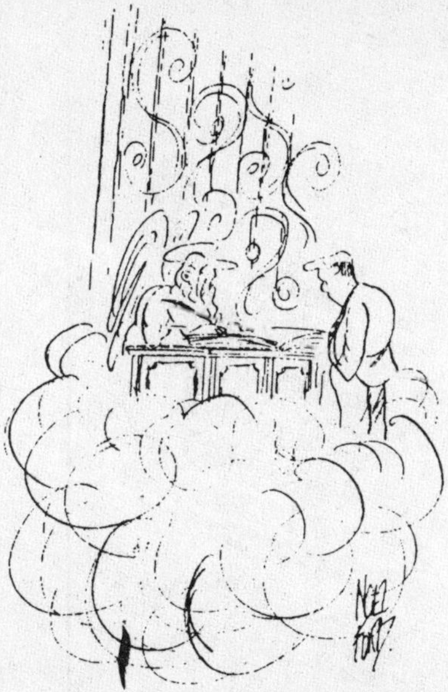

"I'm afraid it's only self-catering these days."

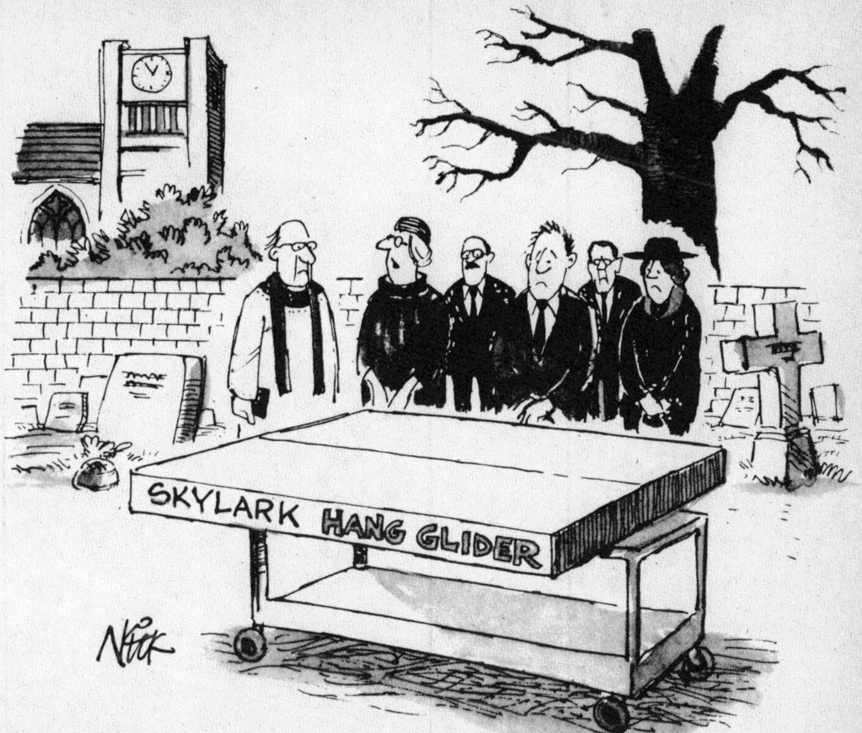

"After the accident, it seemed a shame to waste the carton."

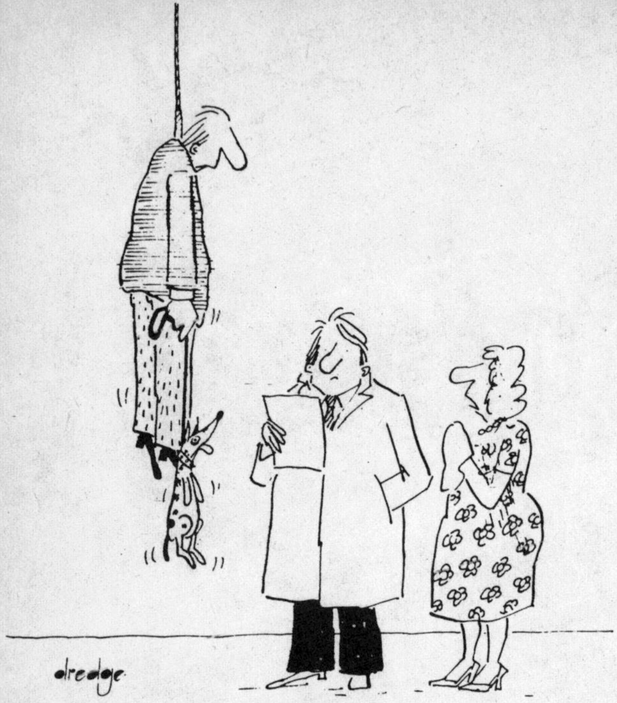

"Harold and Spot were inseparable, Inspector."

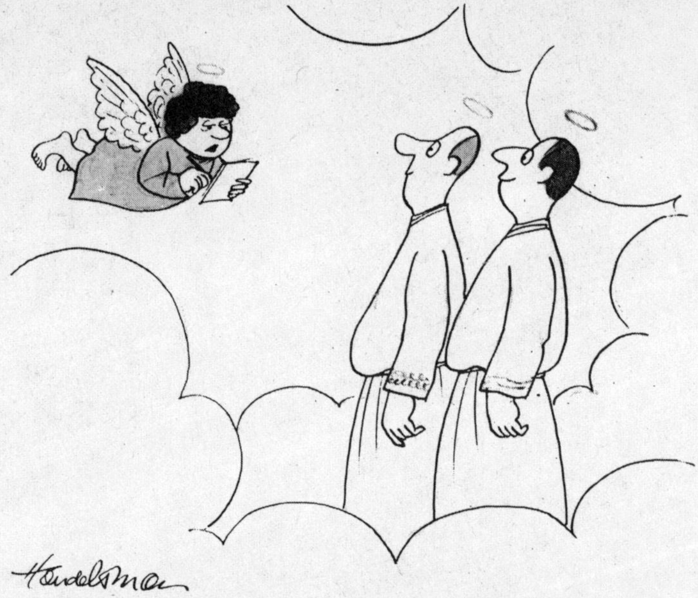

"So that's one nectar and ambrosia, and one nectar and a Western omelette."

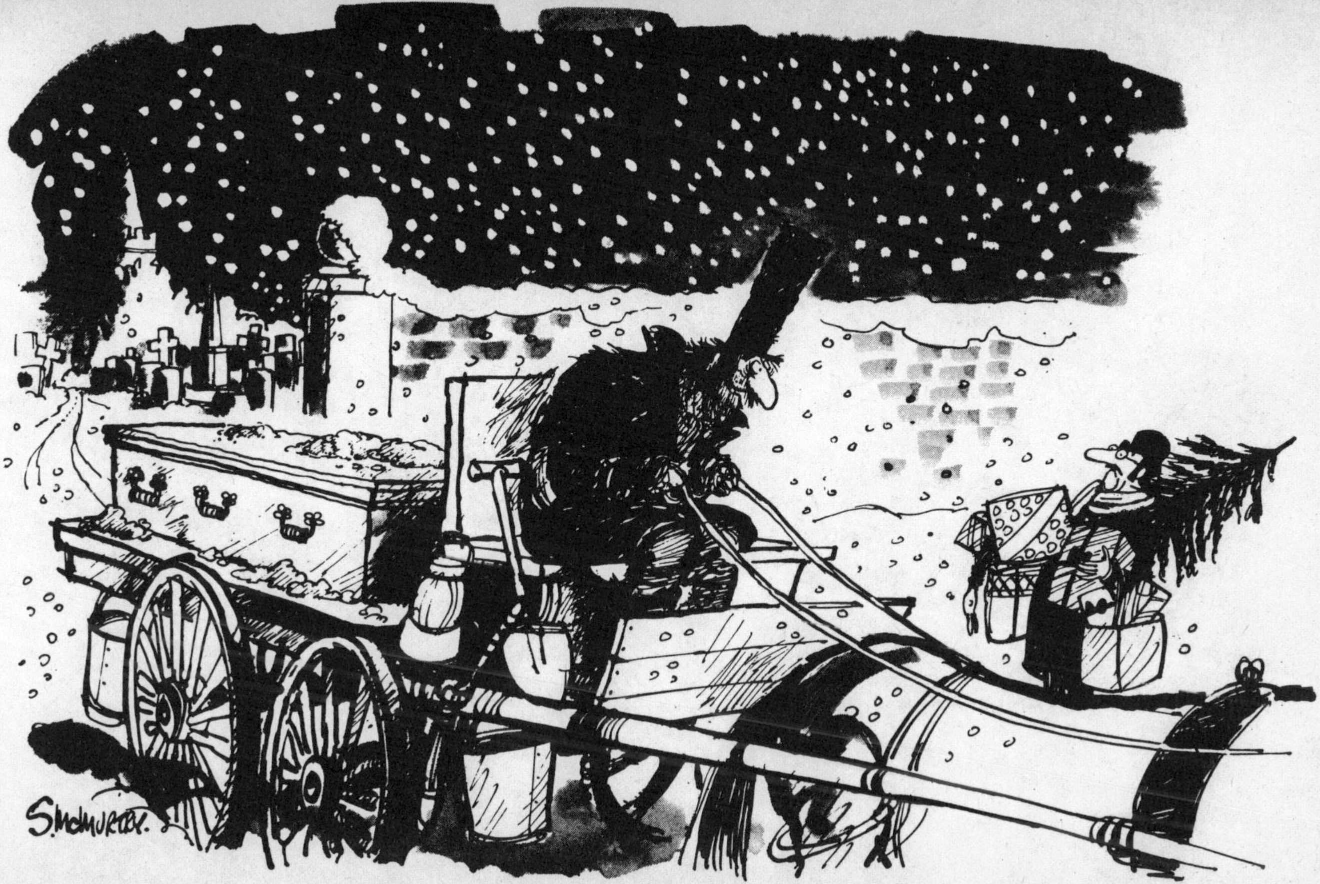

"Not a word to Burke – I want it to be a surprise."

"They take a pretty hard line with tax evaders here."

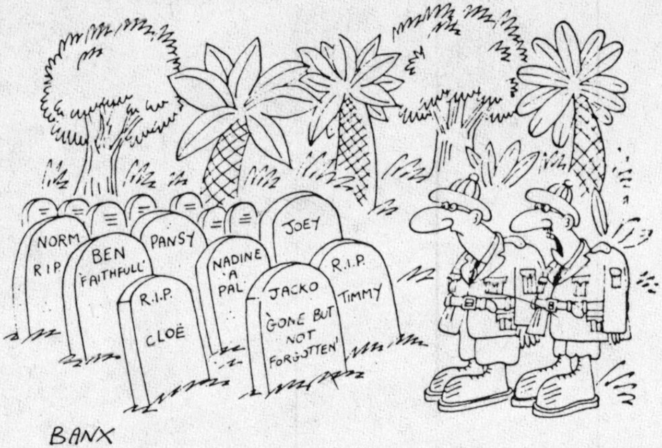

"Not much of an elephants' graveyard though, is it?"

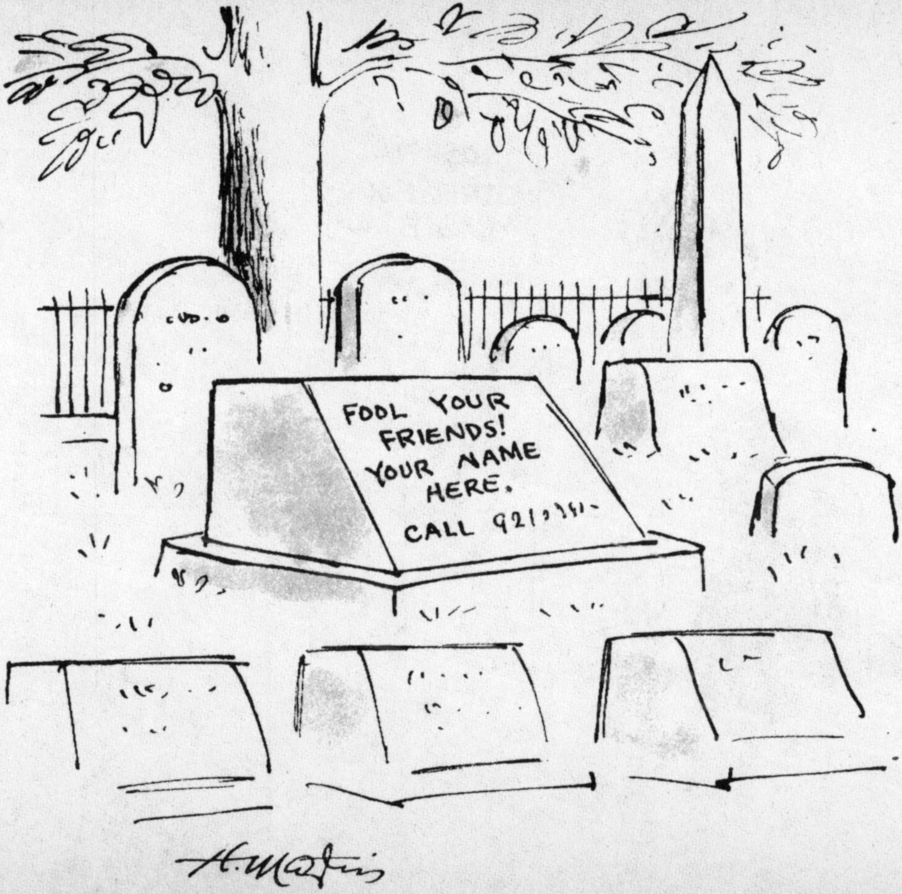
FOOL YOUR FRIENDS!
YOUR NAME HERE.
CALL 921

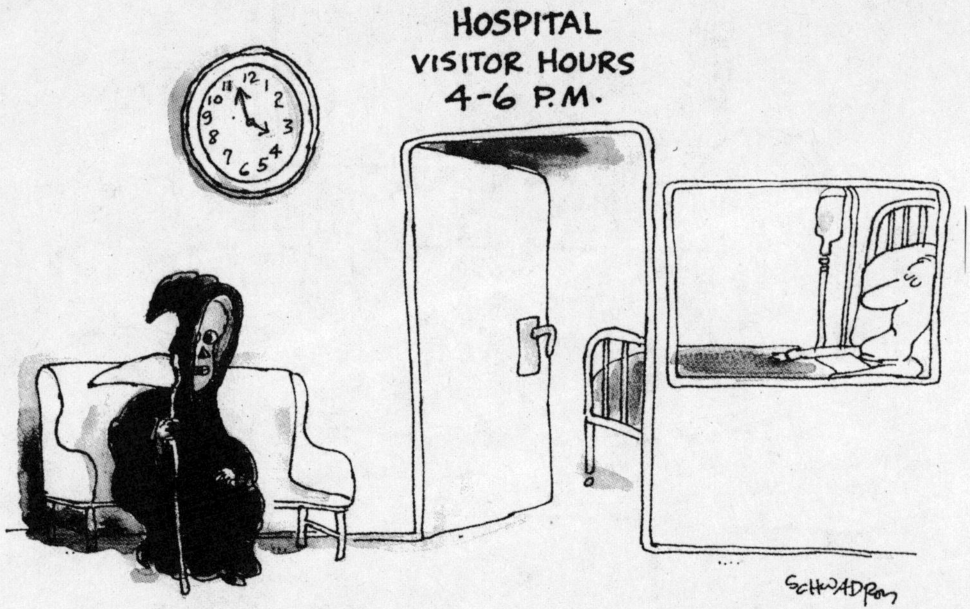
HOSPITAL
VISITOR HOURS
4-6 P.M.
SCHWADRON

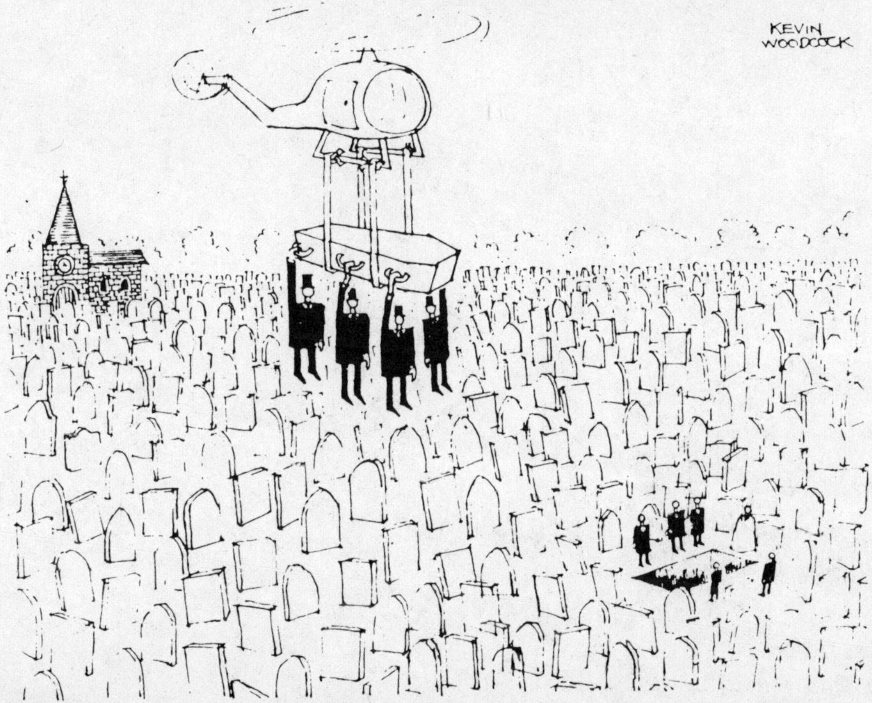
KEVIN
WOODCOCK

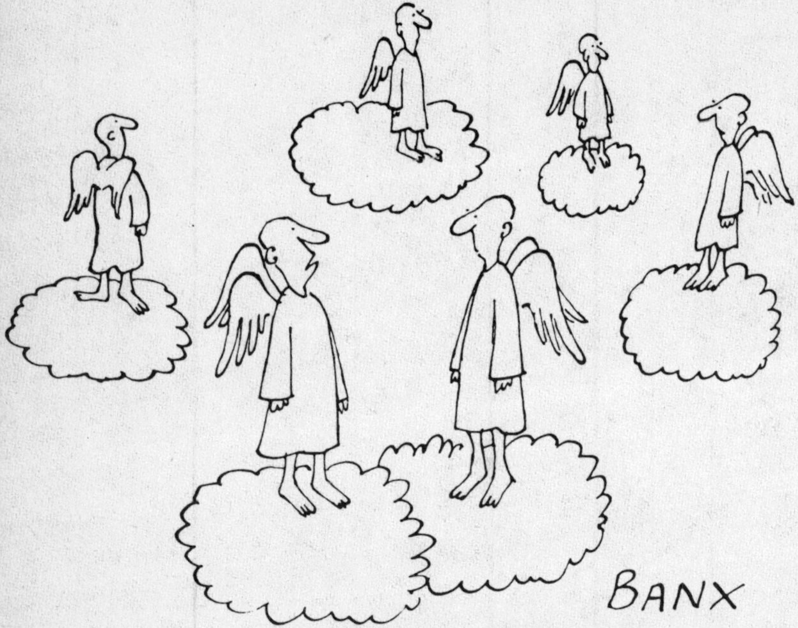

"You know what I miss? Senseless violence."

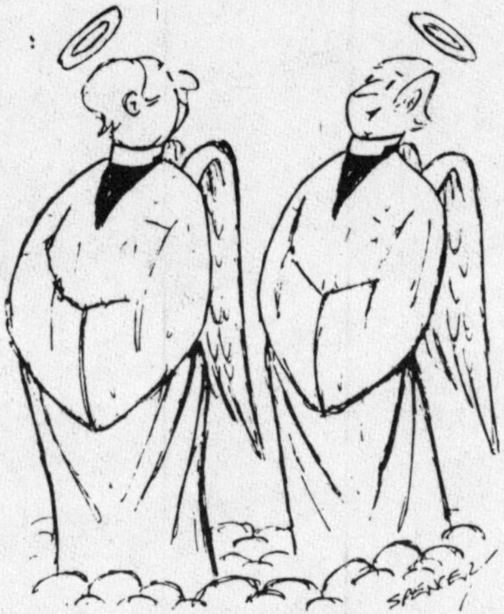

"I suppose this is what they call a business perk . . ."

"Actually, I collapsed while taking part in the East Grimpton Operatic Society's production of 'Faust'."

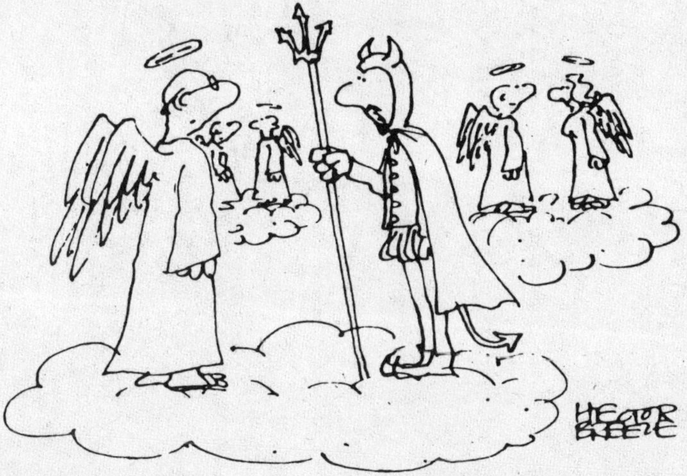

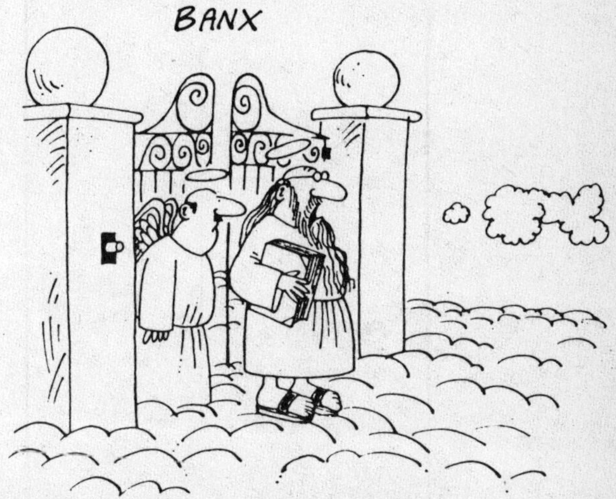

"Bloody agnostics ringing the doorbell again!"

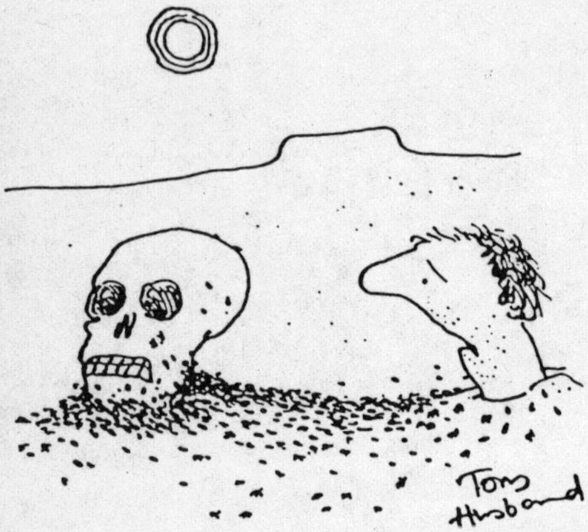

"Pssst, Harry, what's it like?"

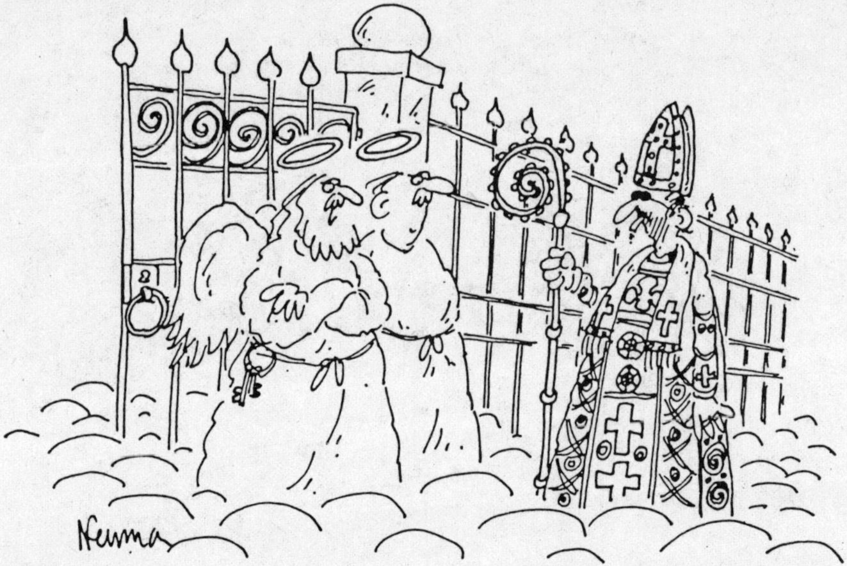

"You always get one or two who try it on."

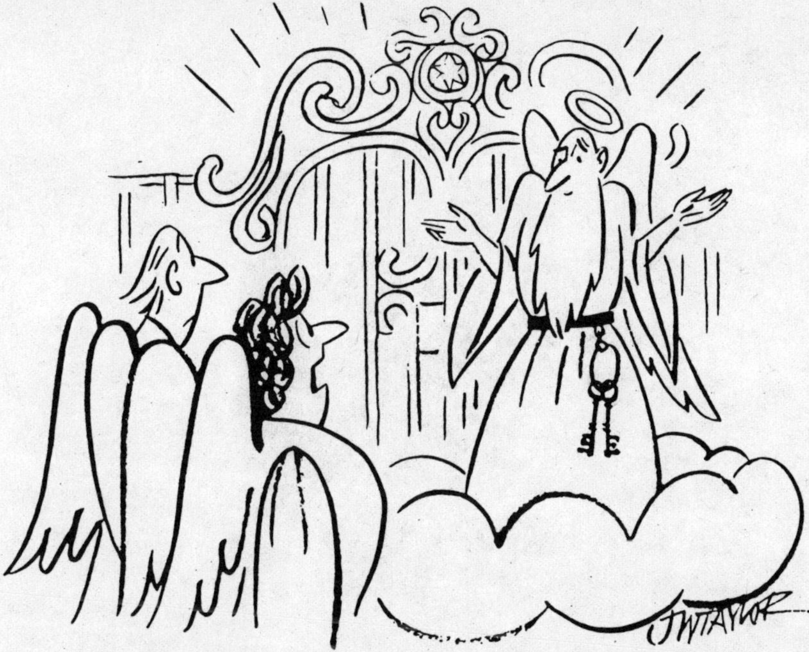

"Well, really! you'd think by now he'd have picked up English."

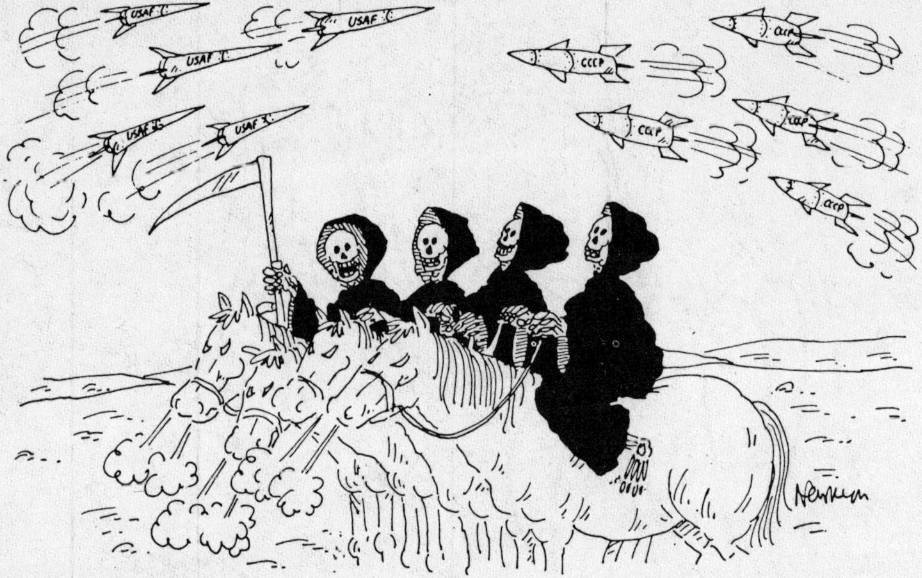

"It's party time!"

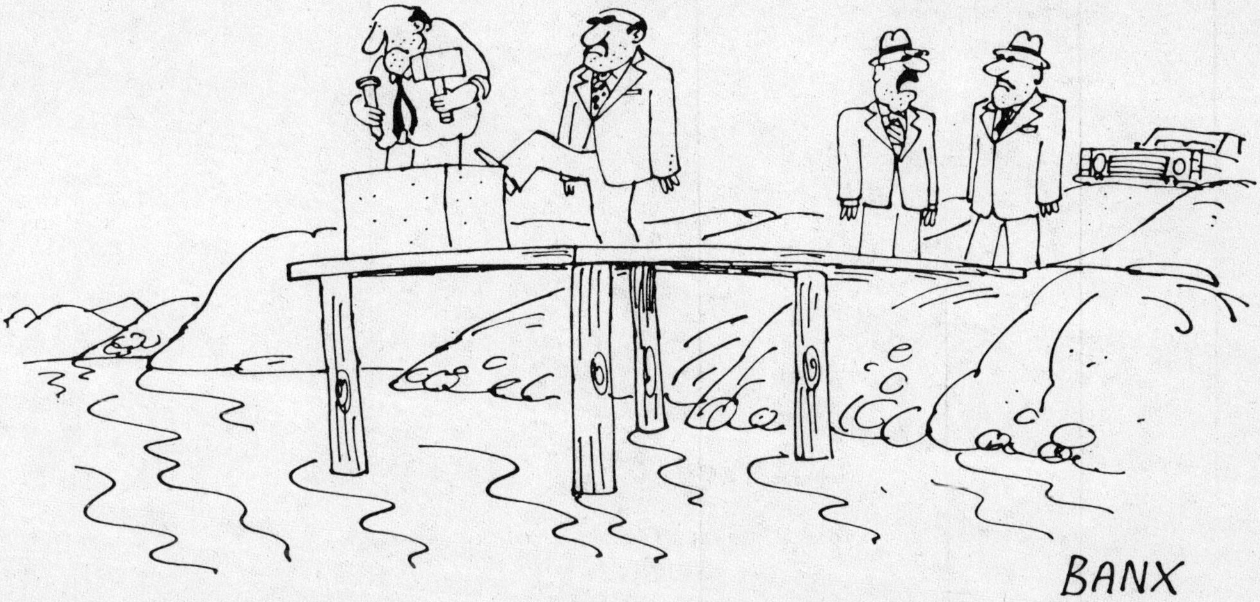

"It's just Mario's sensitive way – he likes to give them a fighting chance."

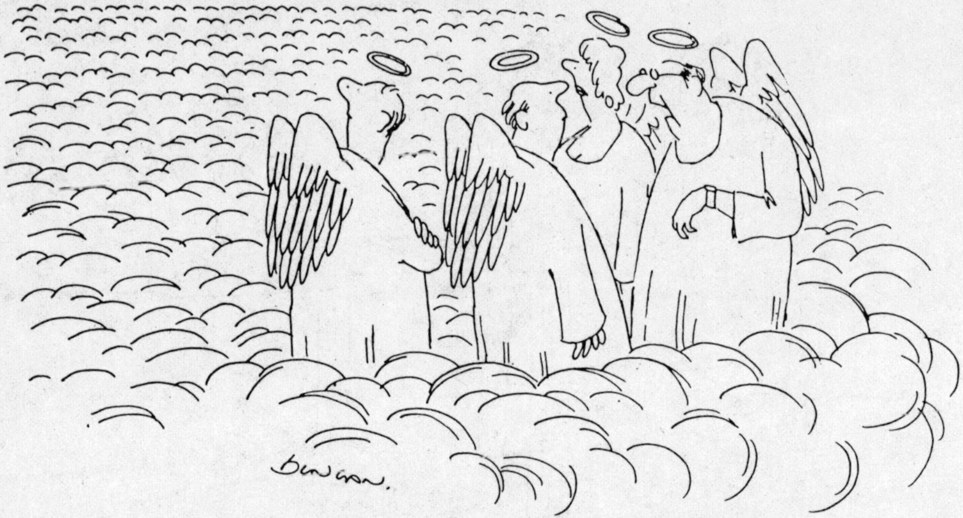

"But if they're not back in 35 minutes, I think we can take it Heaven is flat."

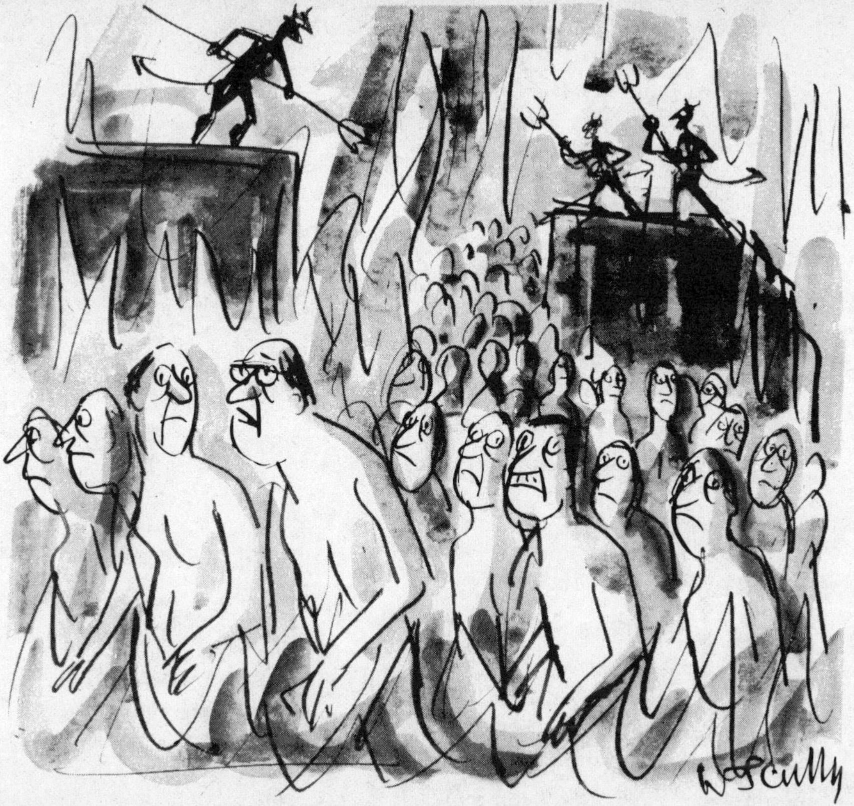

"They tell me it's not even safe to drink the water."

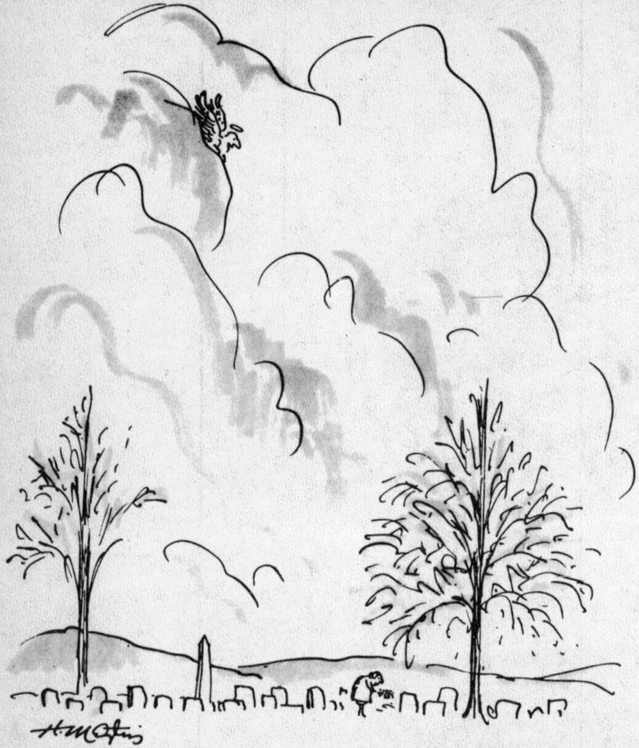

"Midge! Midge! Can't you hear me? It's me, Ernie! Up here! I made it!"

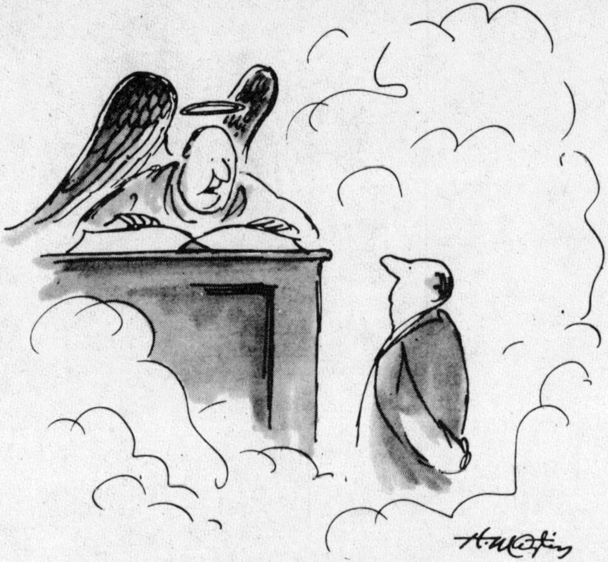

"Well, Mr Arterberry, I see you have done those things you ought to have done except read 'The Mill on the Floss'."

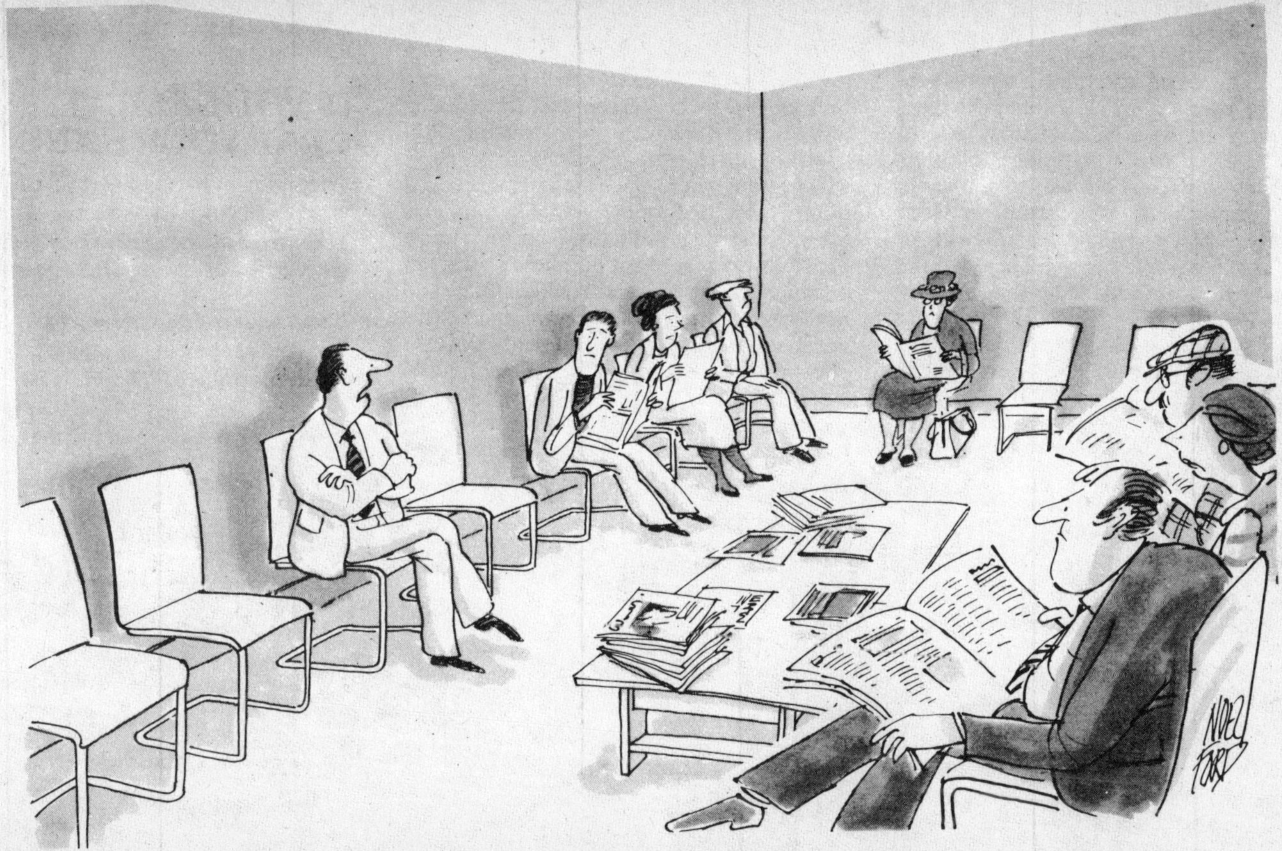

"Somehow, I imagined Limbo would be different."

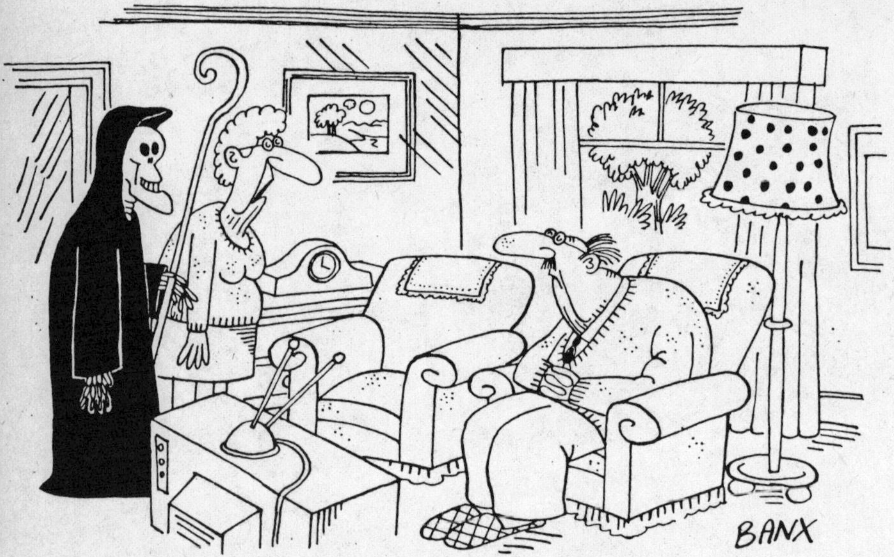

"Apparently most accidents happen in the home, Gordon."

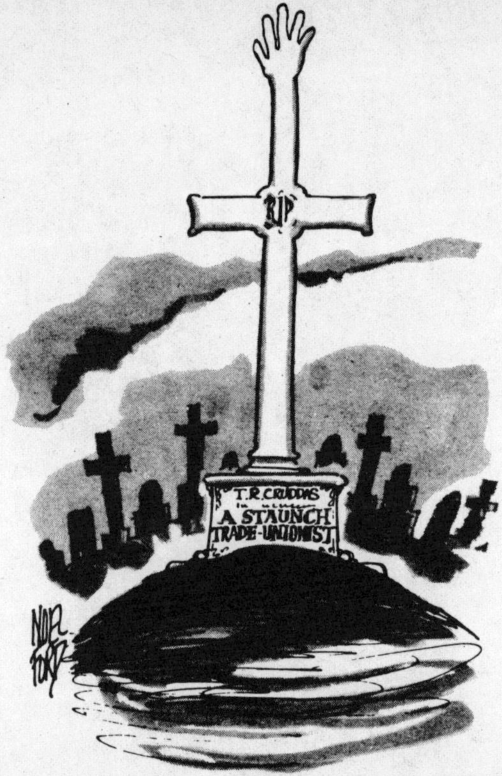

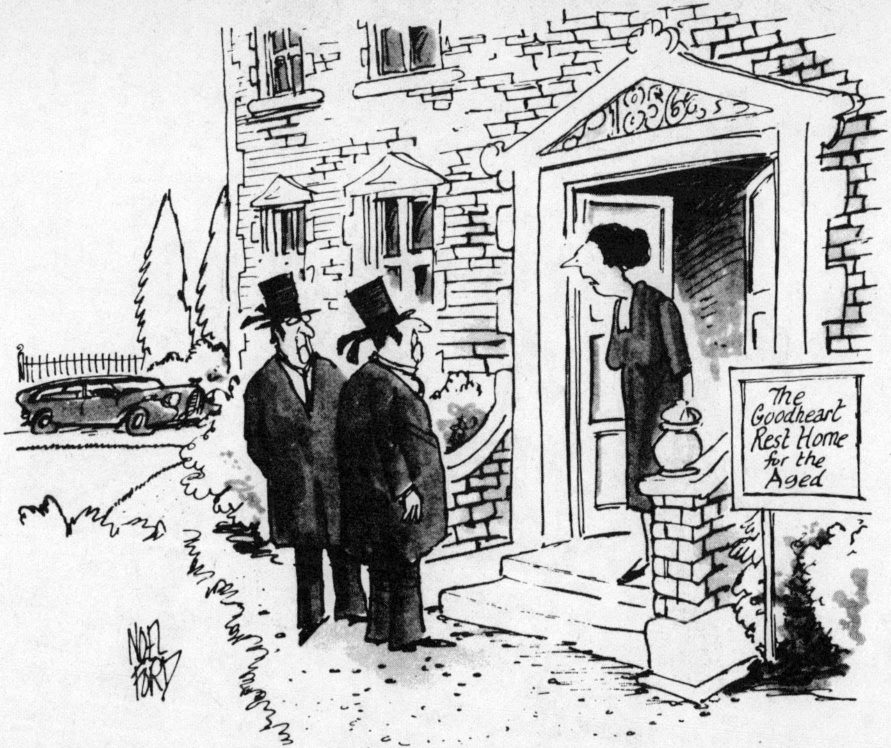

"Nothing for you today."

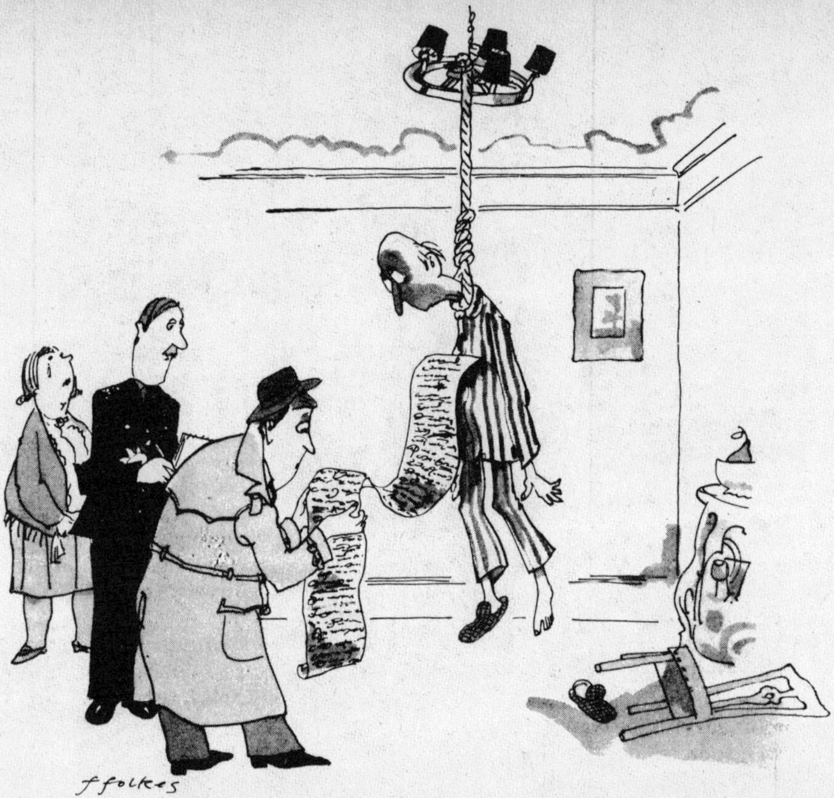

"The gist of it seems to be that his books were too long to get published."

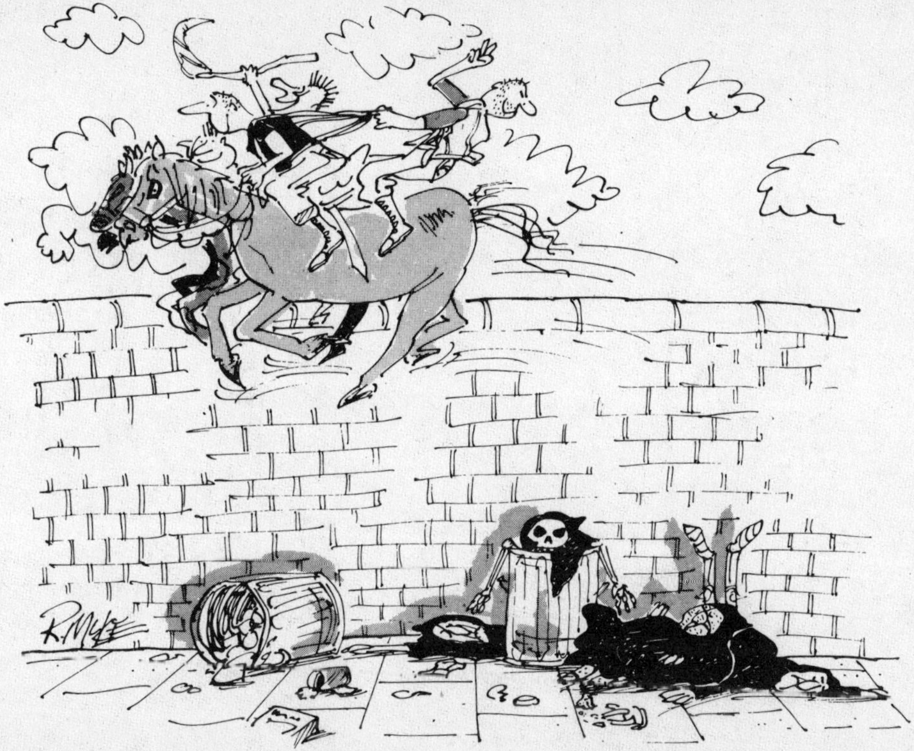

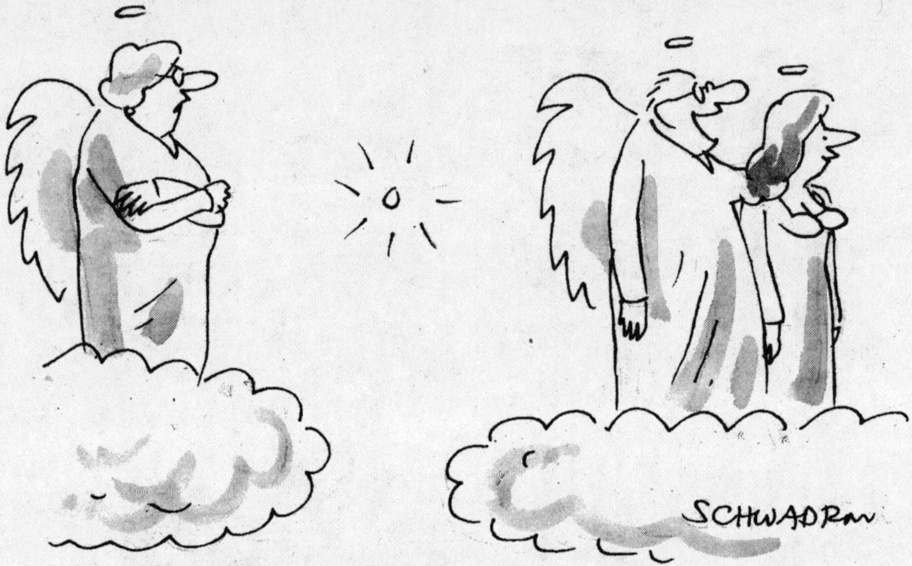

"Our vow said, 'Till death us do part', so that settles that, Agnes."

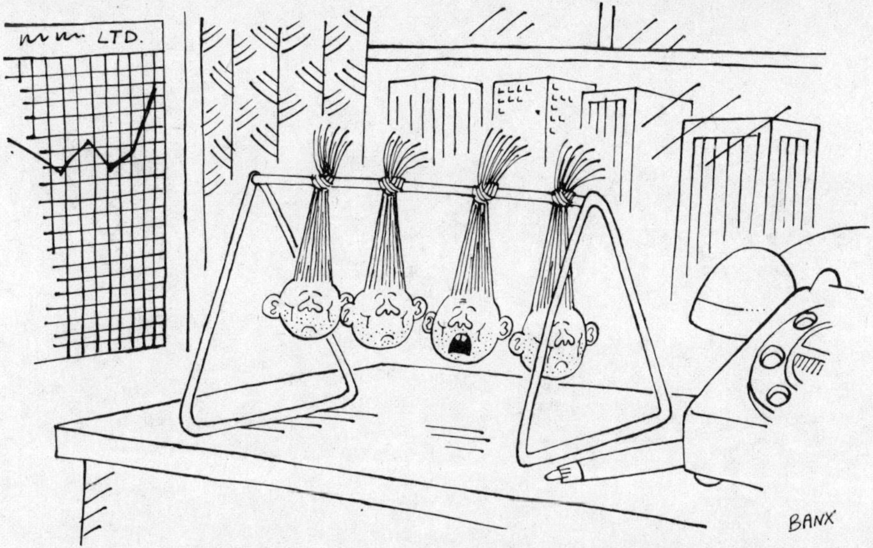

"You'd think things would've changed a bit once we got Overseas Aid."

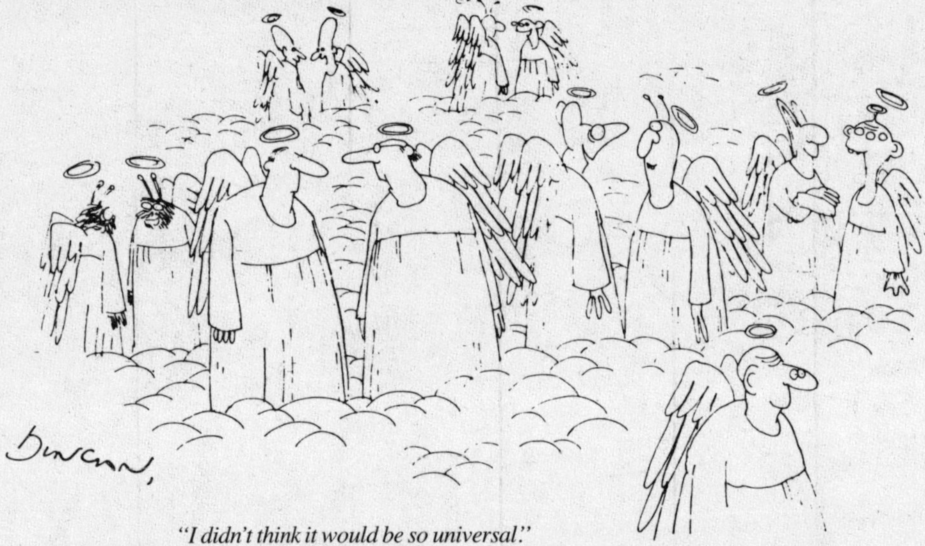

"I didn't think it would be so universal."

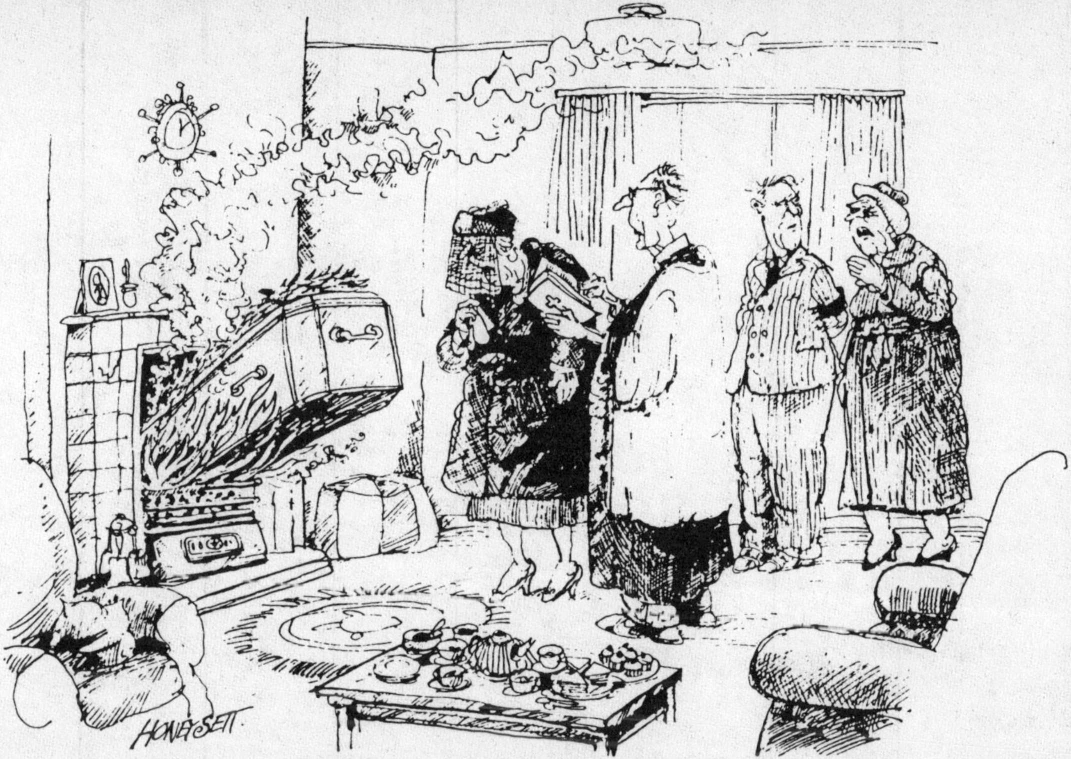

"There'll be trouble over this – impersonating a vicar."

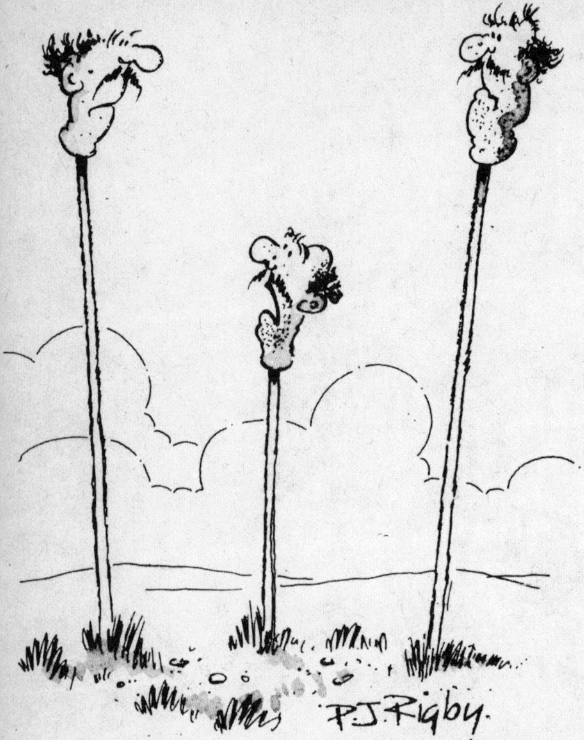

"The bastards even remembered I was only four feet six inches."

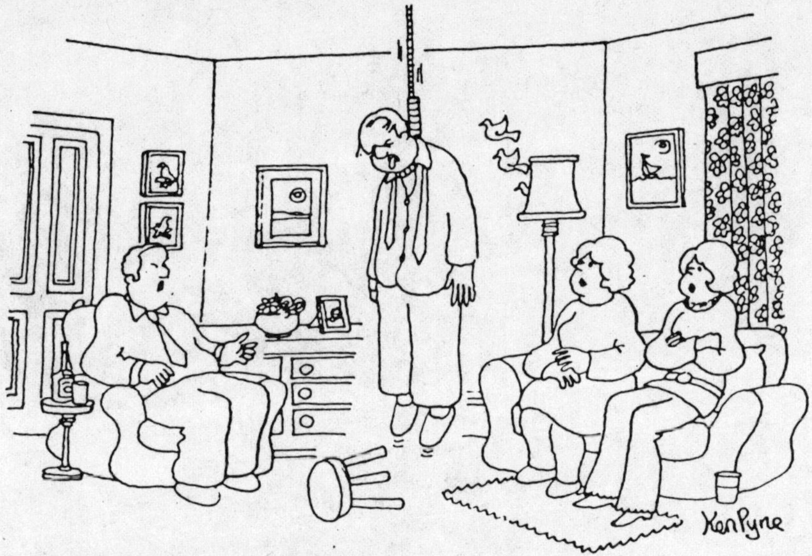

"He didn't tell us if it's a play, a film or a book."

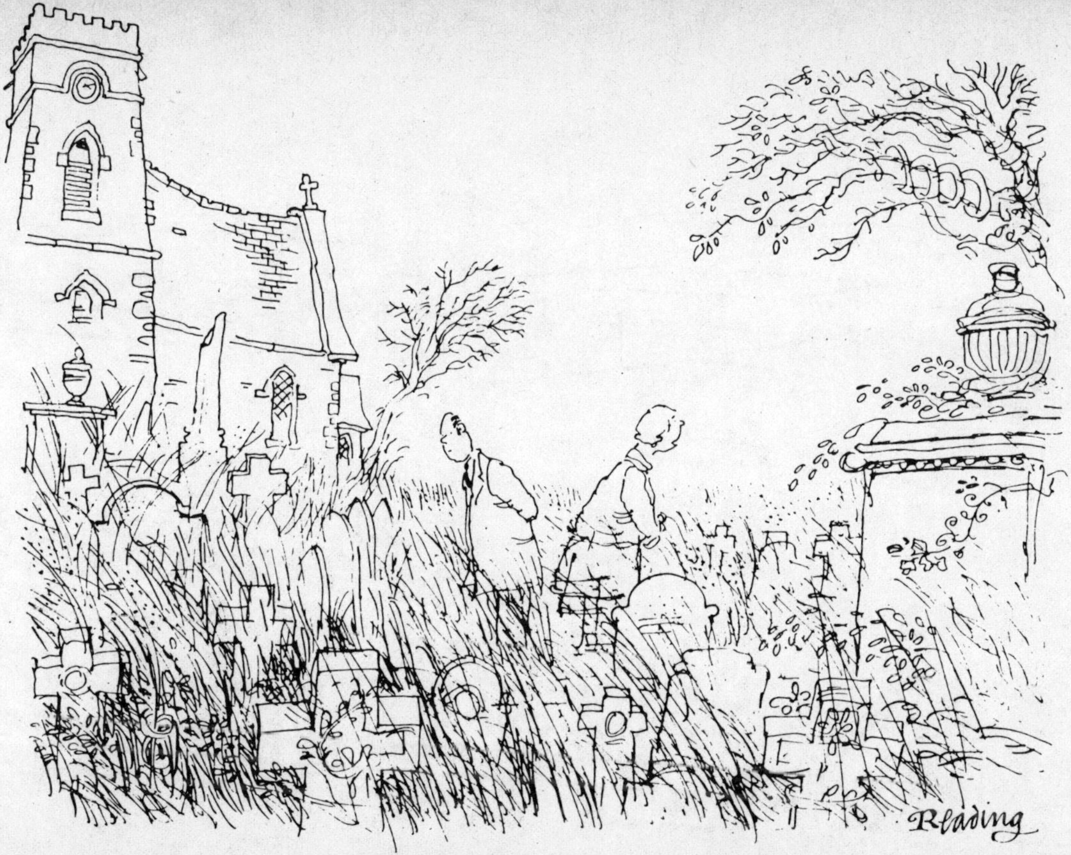

"I know it's here somewhere – it says 'Gone but not forgotten'."

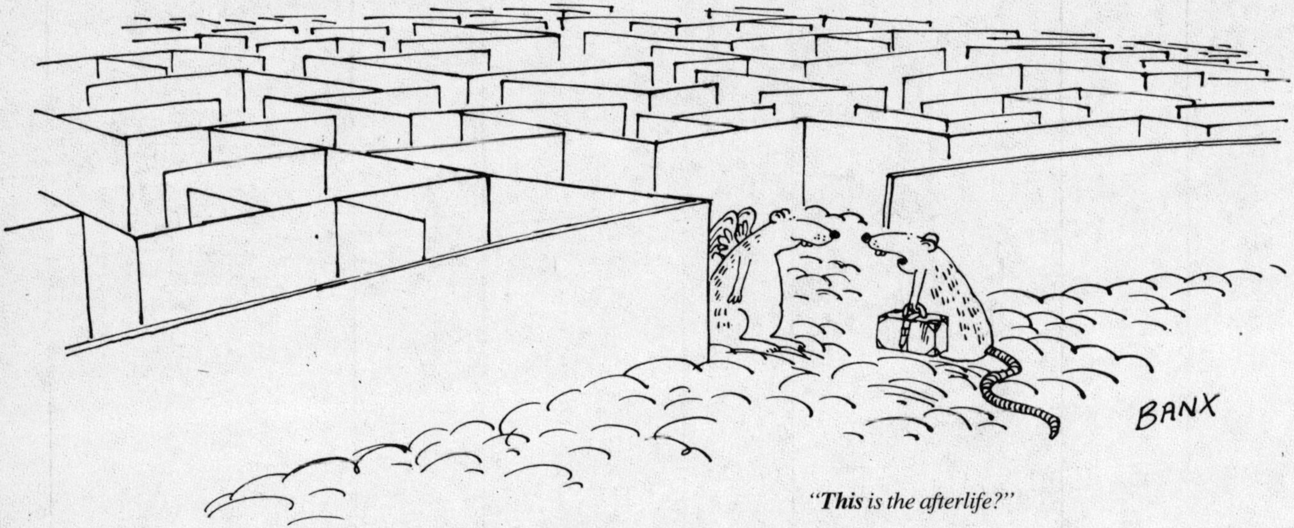

"***This*** *is the afterlife?"*

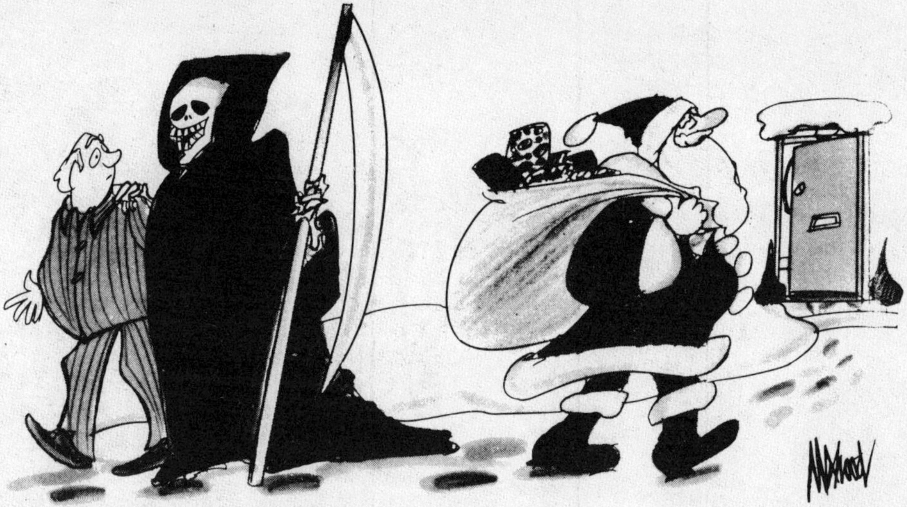

"I bet you didn't believe in him, either!"

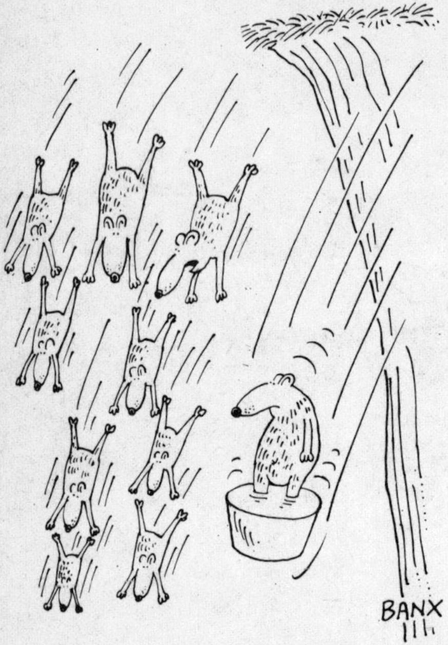

"I suppose it was only a matter of time before the Mafia muscled in."

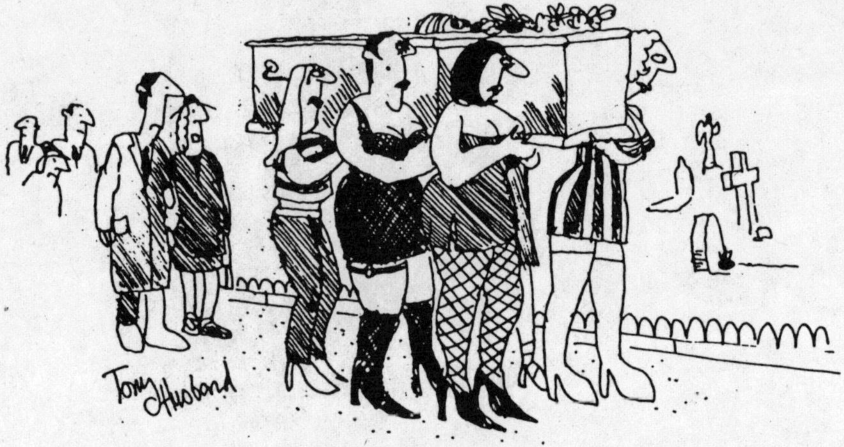

"Apparently, they're friends of your father's from the golf club."

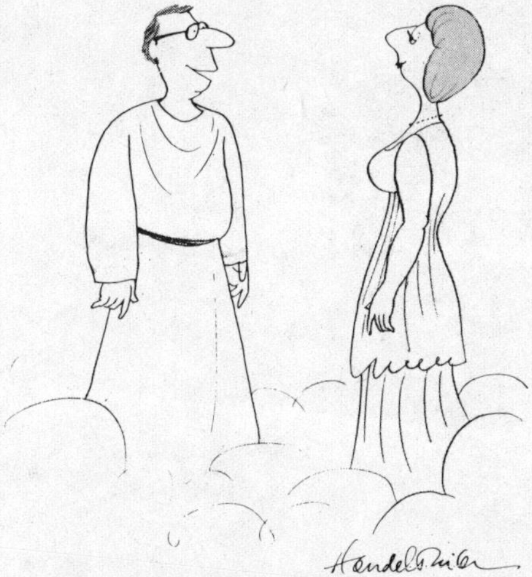

"May I say how much I admire the care you take with your appearance? So many dead women just let themselves go."

"And in keeping with a will full of surprises – my client's dying wish . . ."

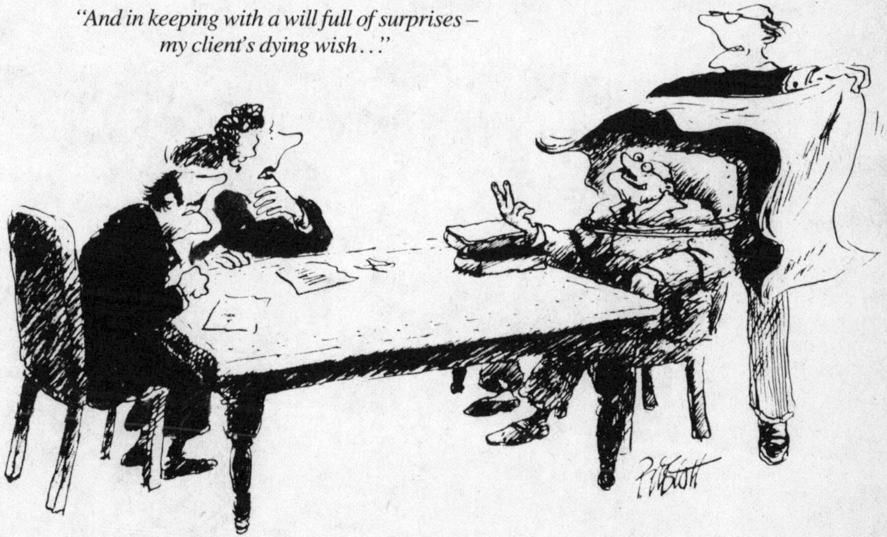

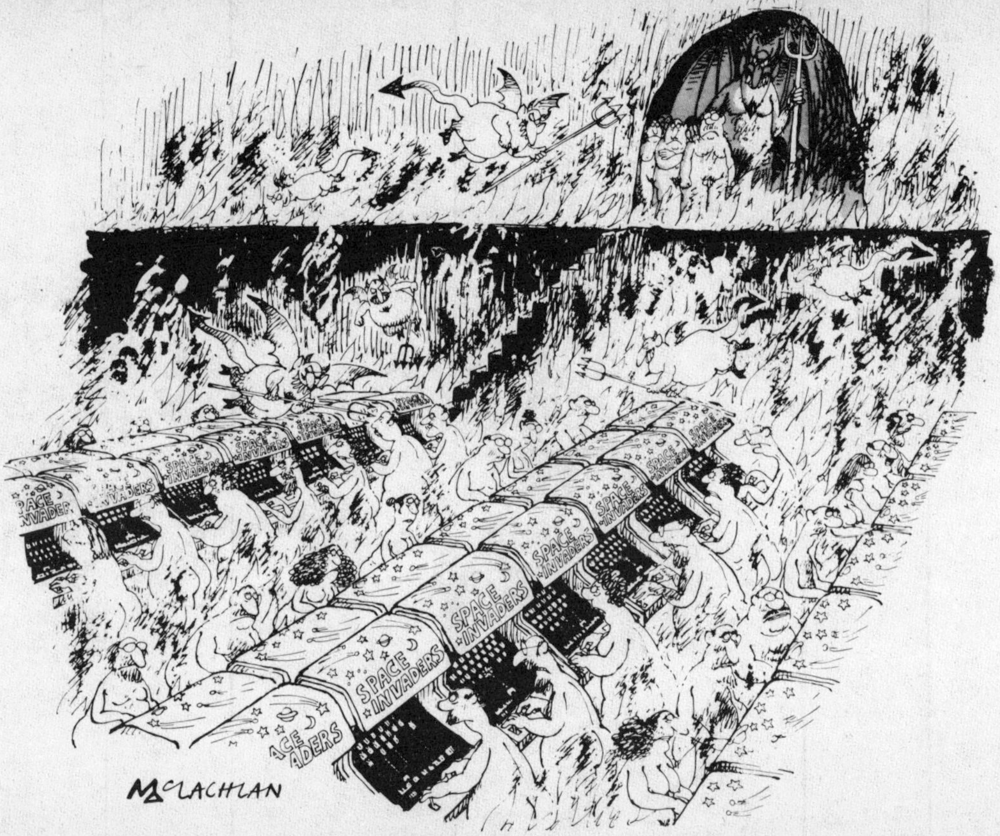
SPACE INVADERS
McLACHLAN

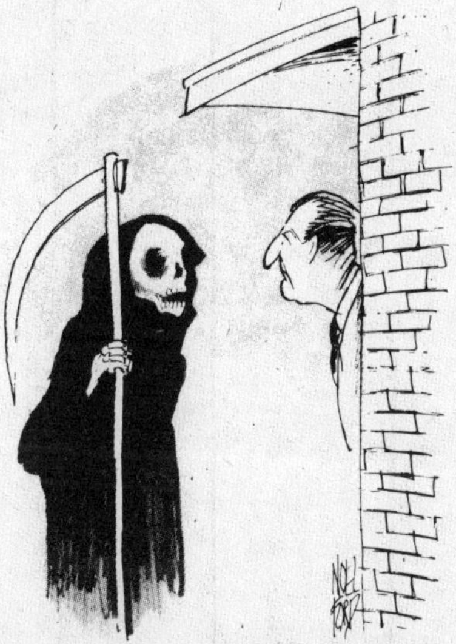

"Look, I'm sorry, mate – I'm only doing my bloody job, aren't I?"

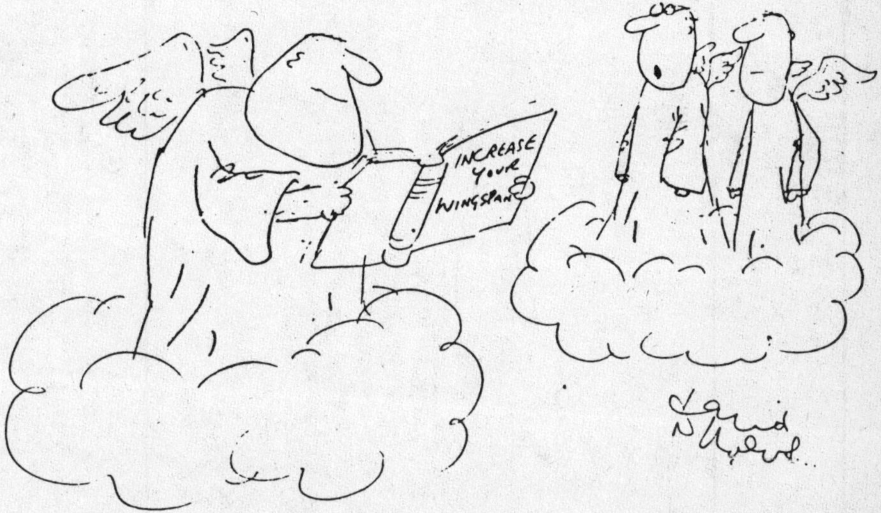

"He was always crazy about body building."

"It may be regarded as somewhat primitive, but at least it makes a change from those ruddy peanuts."

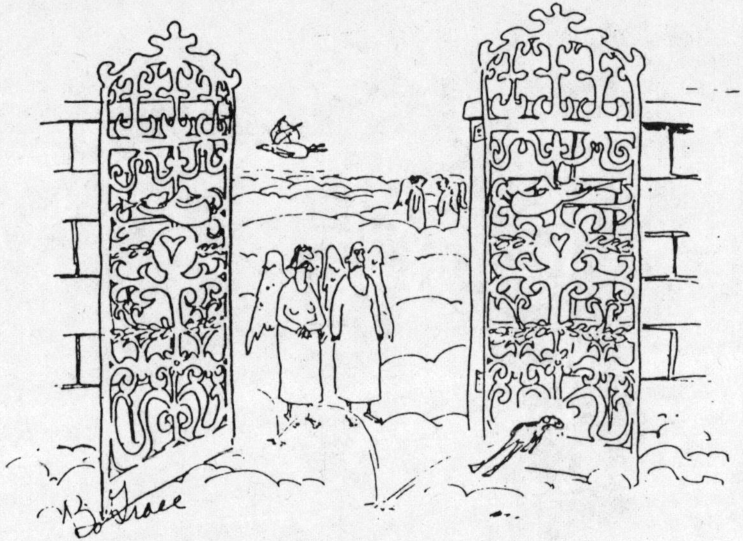

"Poor Nigel. I begged him not to convert to Hinduism."

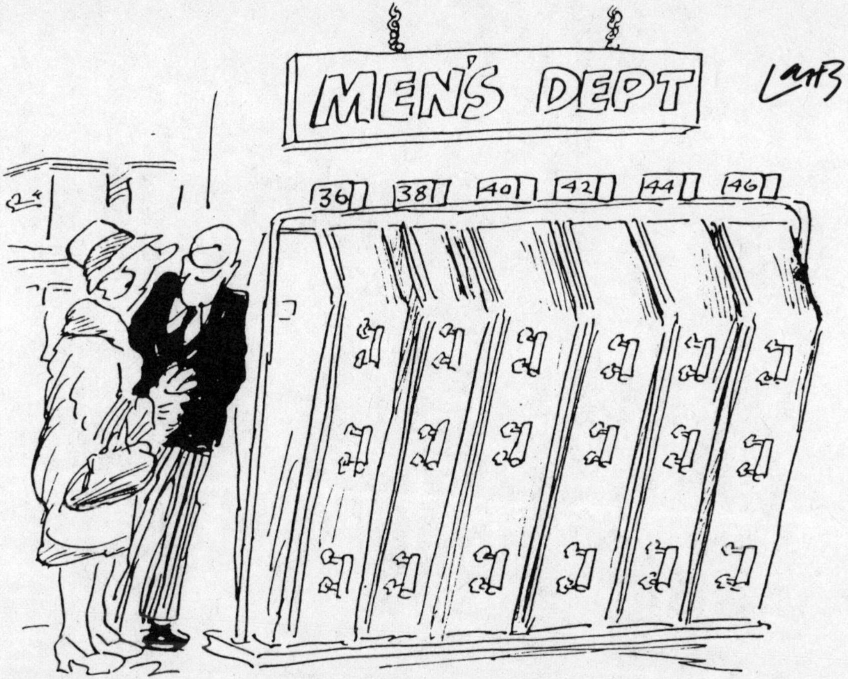

MEN'S DEPT
36
38
40
42
44
46

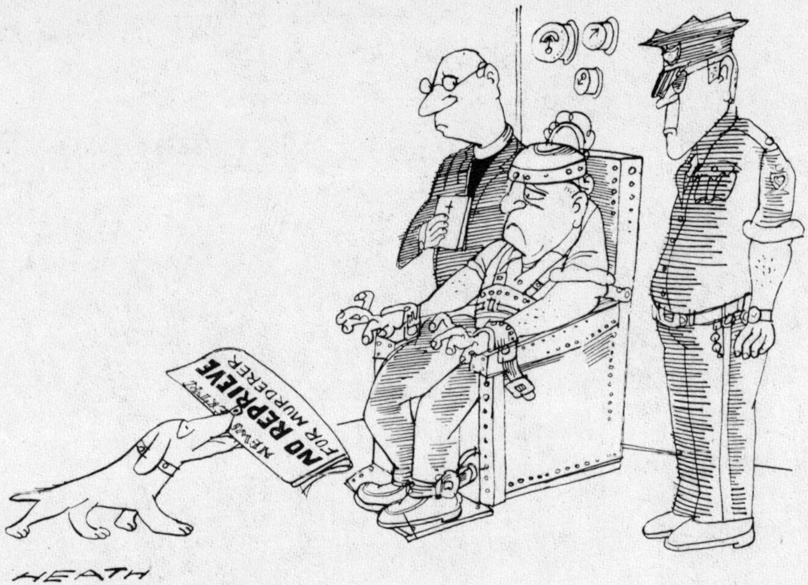
NEWS
NO REPRIEVE
FOR MURDERER
HEATH

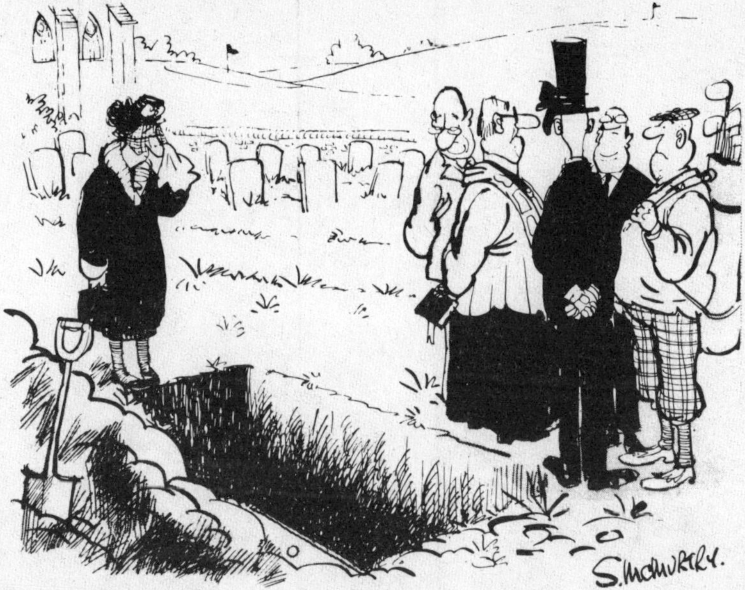

"Well, I say one club's length from the ball with a one stroke penalty."

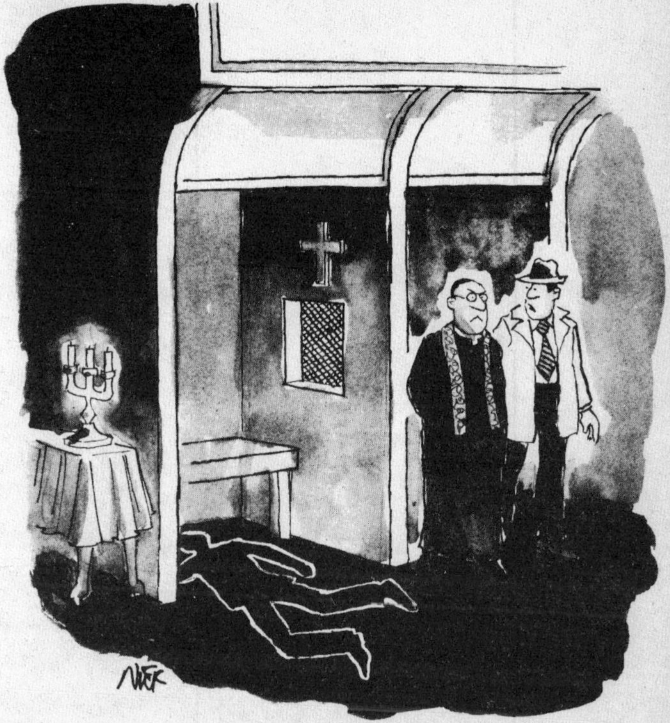

"That must have been some sin, father..."

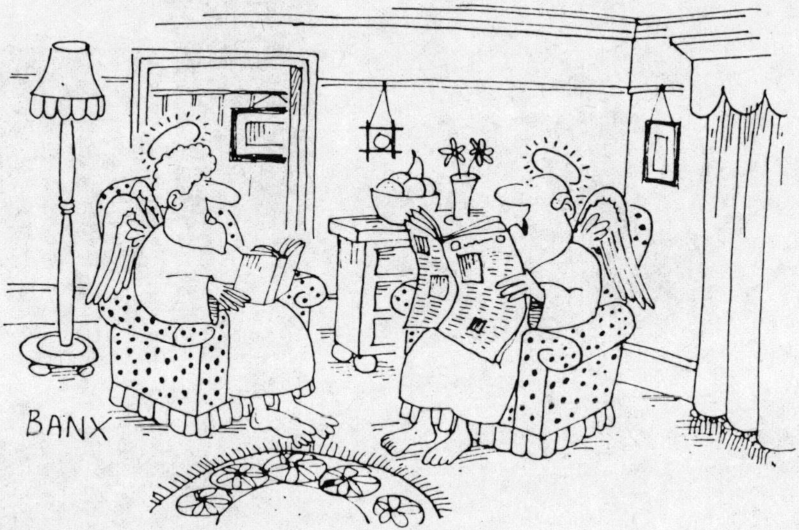

"I said, I do believe we've been struck by a neutron bomb."

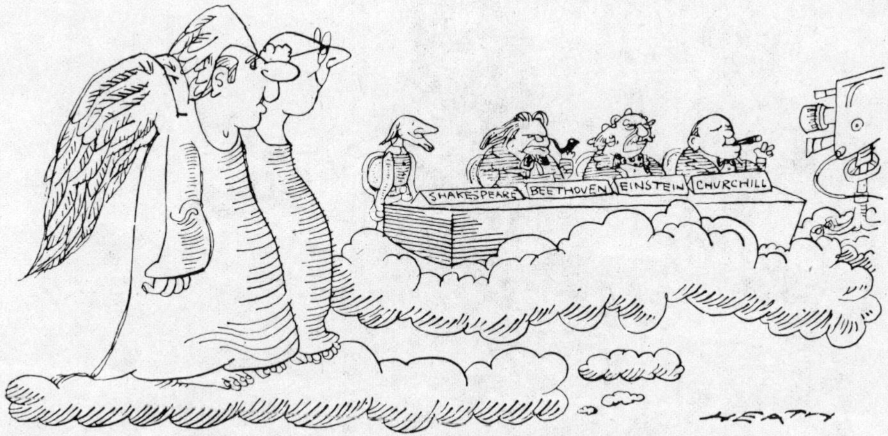

"Mind you, TV panel games seem to be more fun up here."

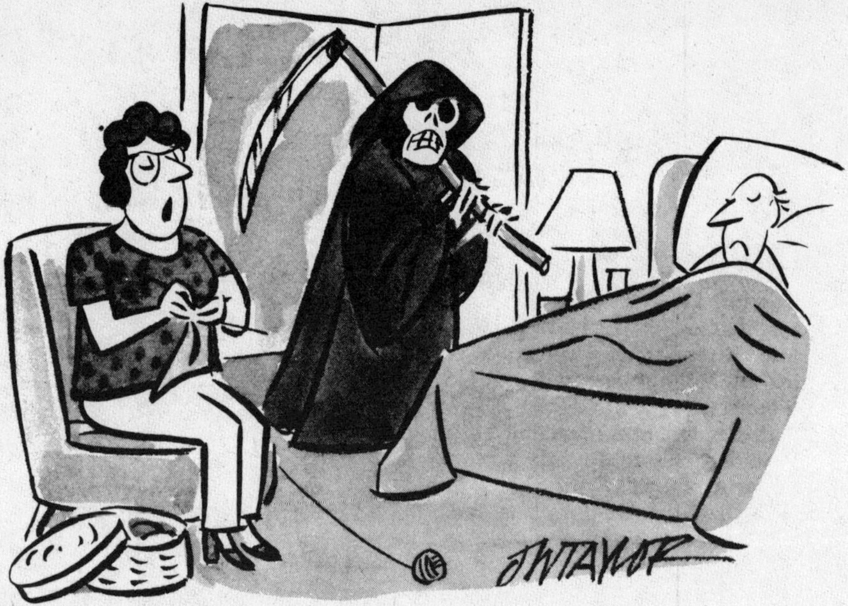

"On your way out could you just go over the front lawn?"

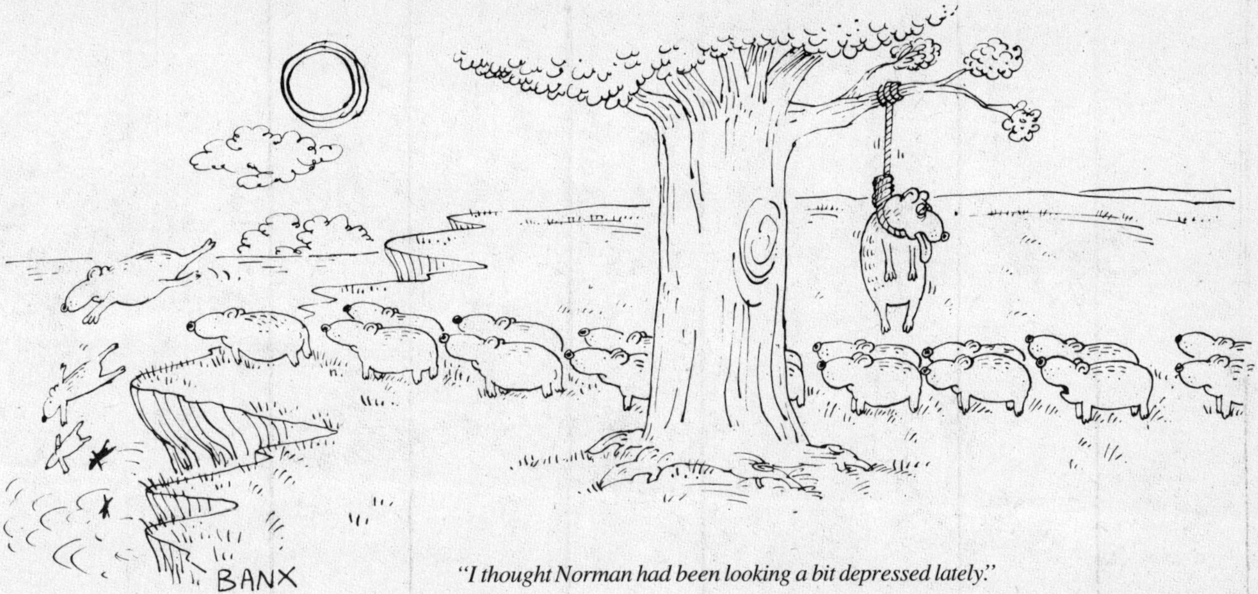

"I thought Norman had been looking a bit depressed lately."

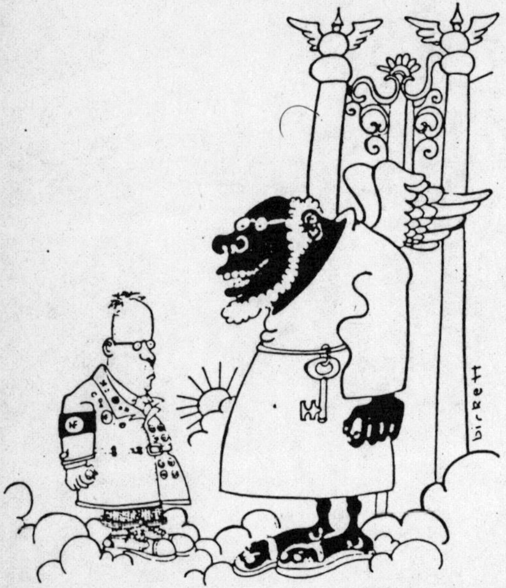

"Actually, there **was** a vacancy, but it was filled a few minutes ago."

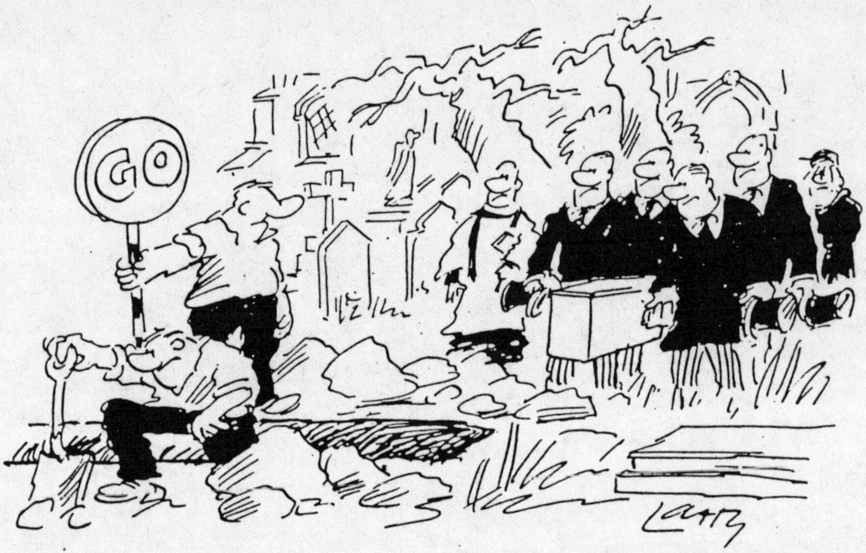

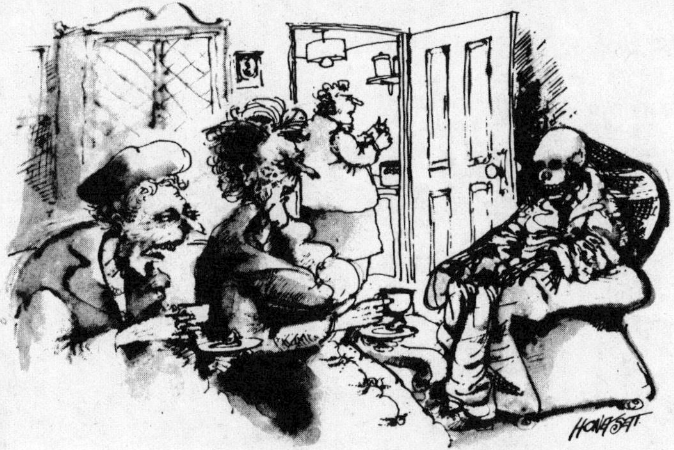

"I know they never really got on but she could at least dust him now and again."

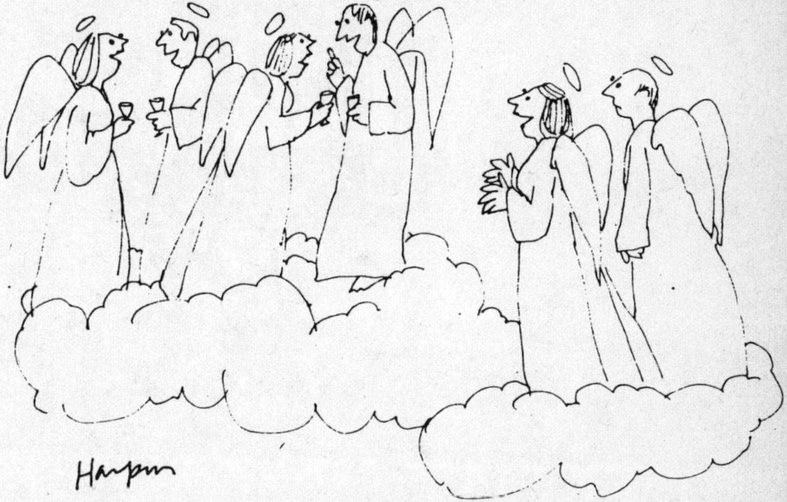

"Oh, super – aprés life!"

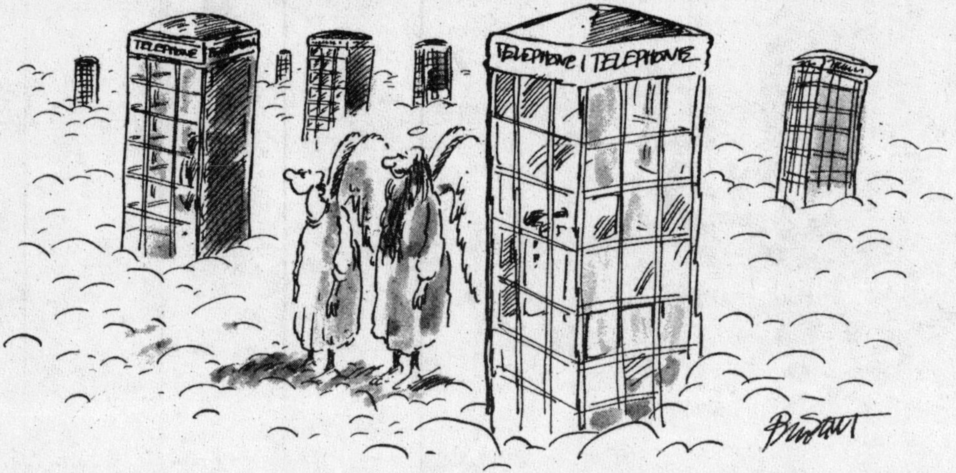

"And they all work?"

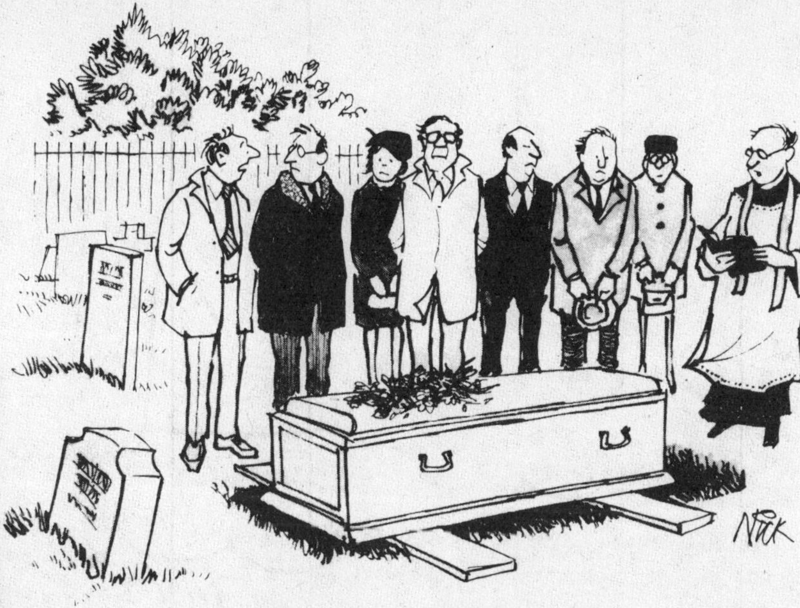

"It was a terrible shock. I thought he died years ago."

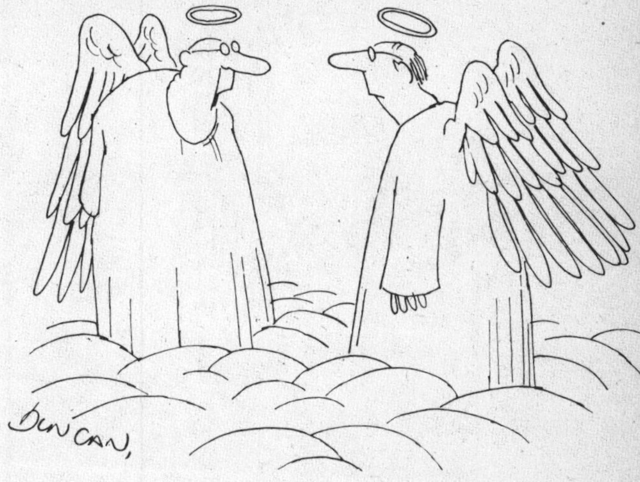

"Mind you, I had hoped to have met a few more famous dead people by now."

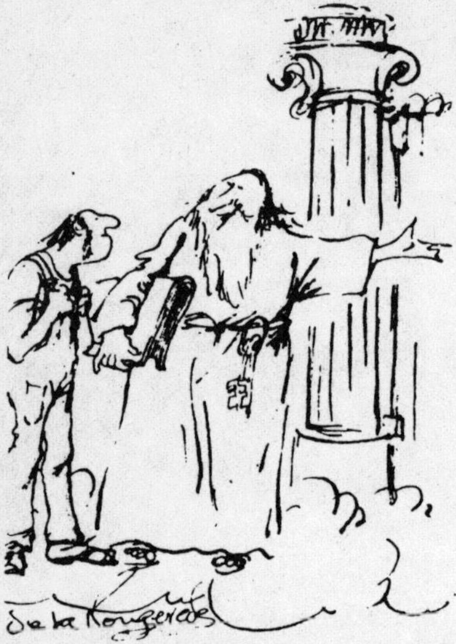

"I think we can dispense with the formalities, for a plumber."

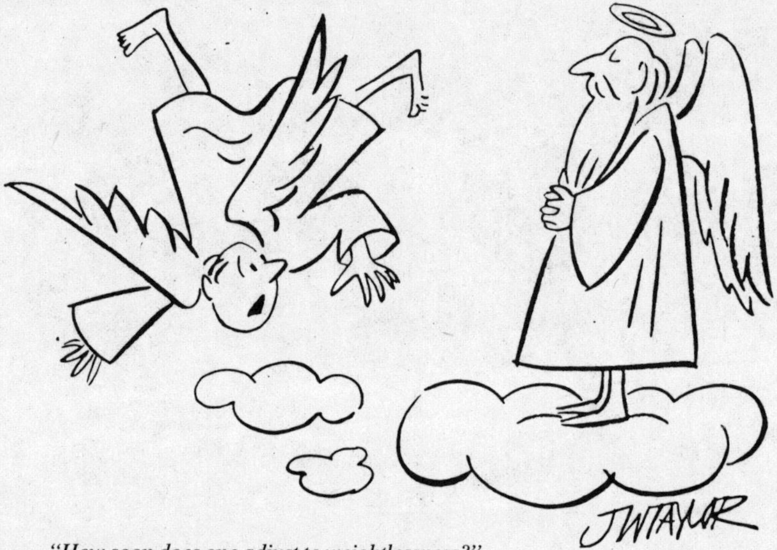

"How soon does one adjust to weightlessness?"

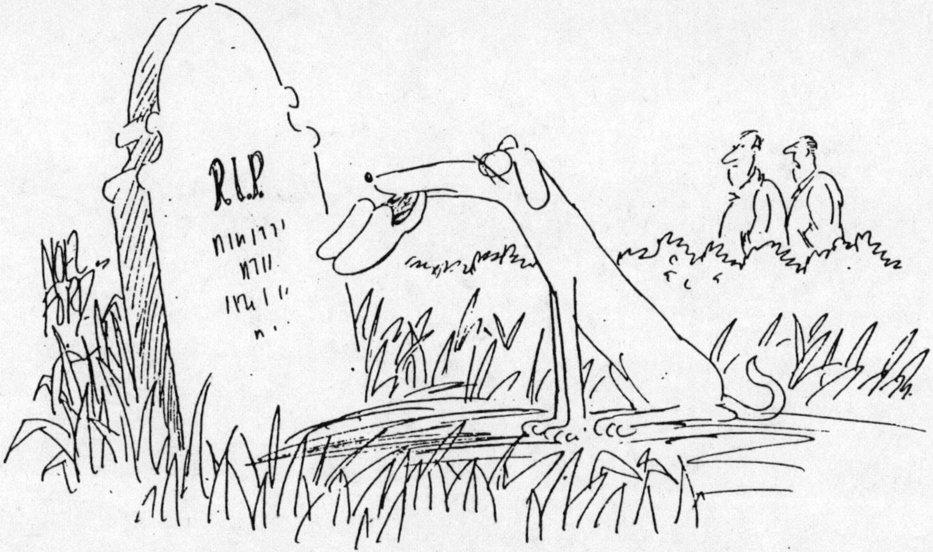

"No, no – he's not devoted, just stupid."

*"I never imagined Hell would be **this** bad."*

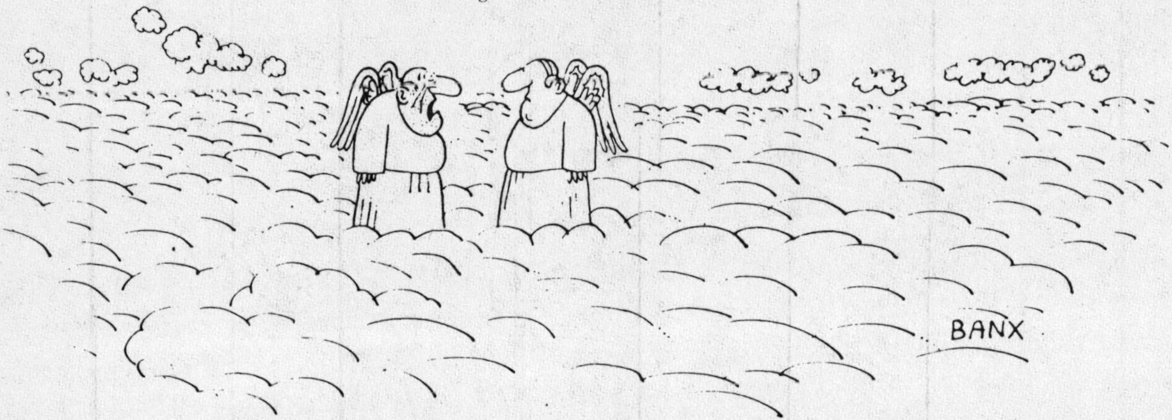

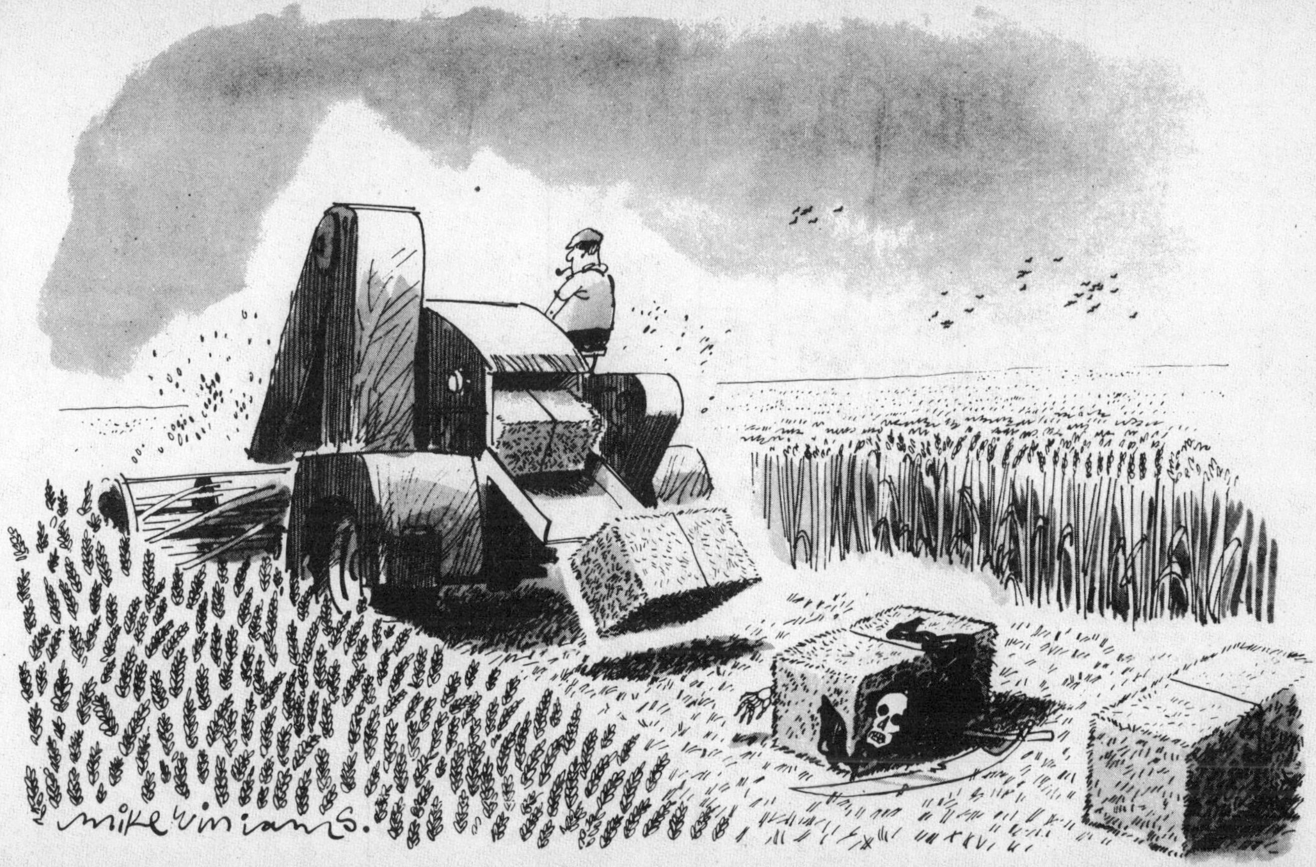
mike williams.

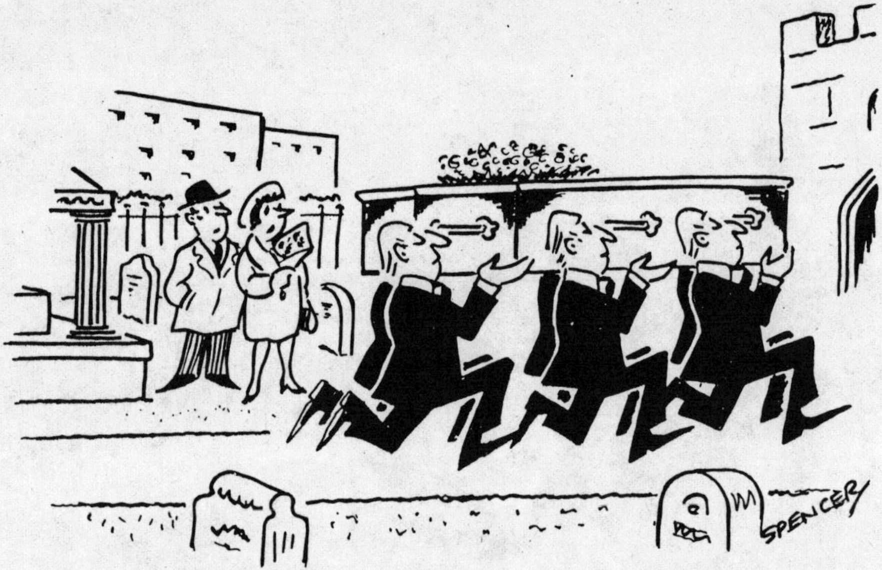

"Another middle-aged jogger, I suppose."

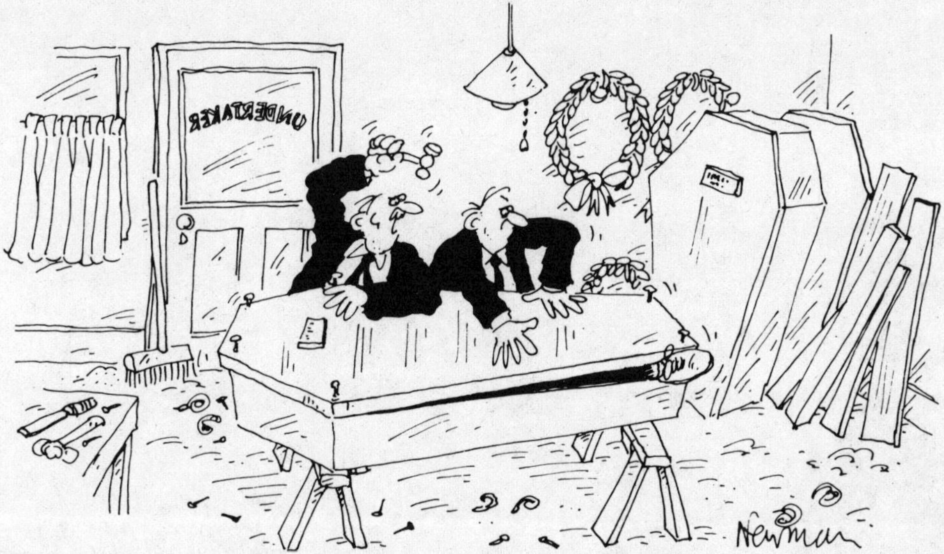

"Bloody salesmen always give us trouble."

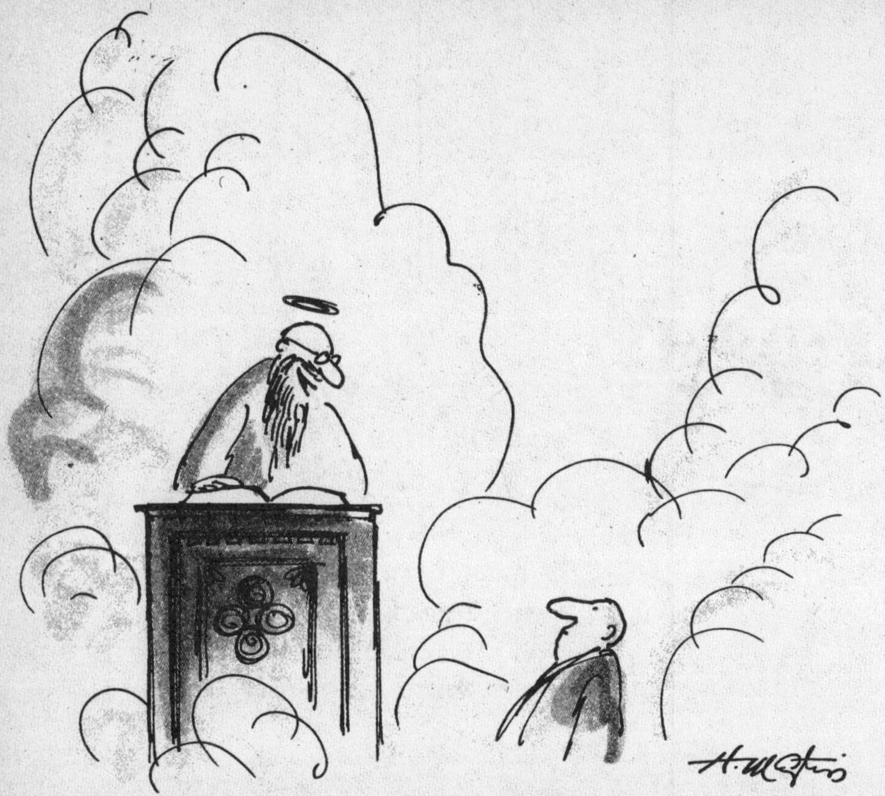

"I thought you'd like to know that the day after you died you won a $22.5 million lottery."

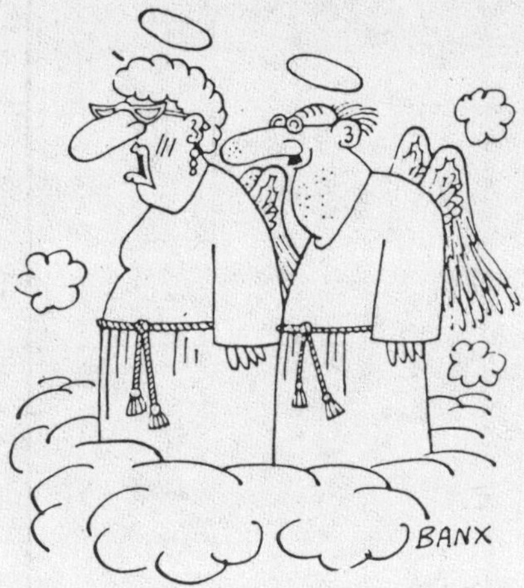

"Do you have to go around showing everyone your autopsy scar?"

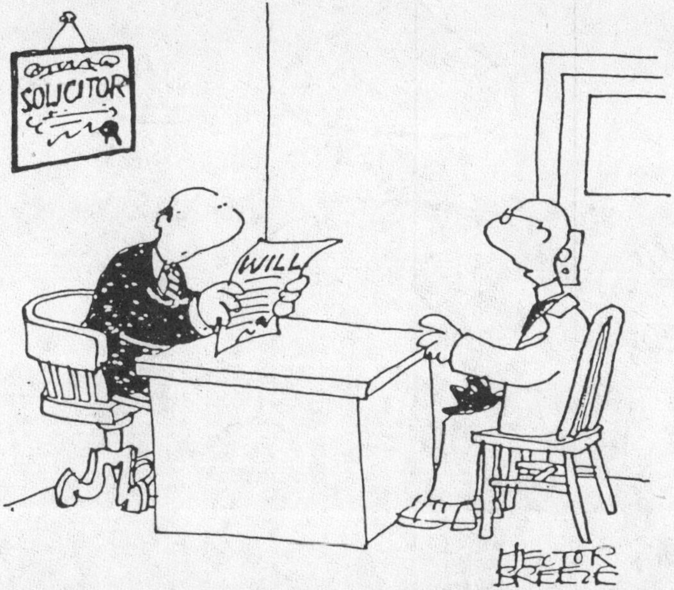

"I suppose it wouldn't by any chance be the earth?"

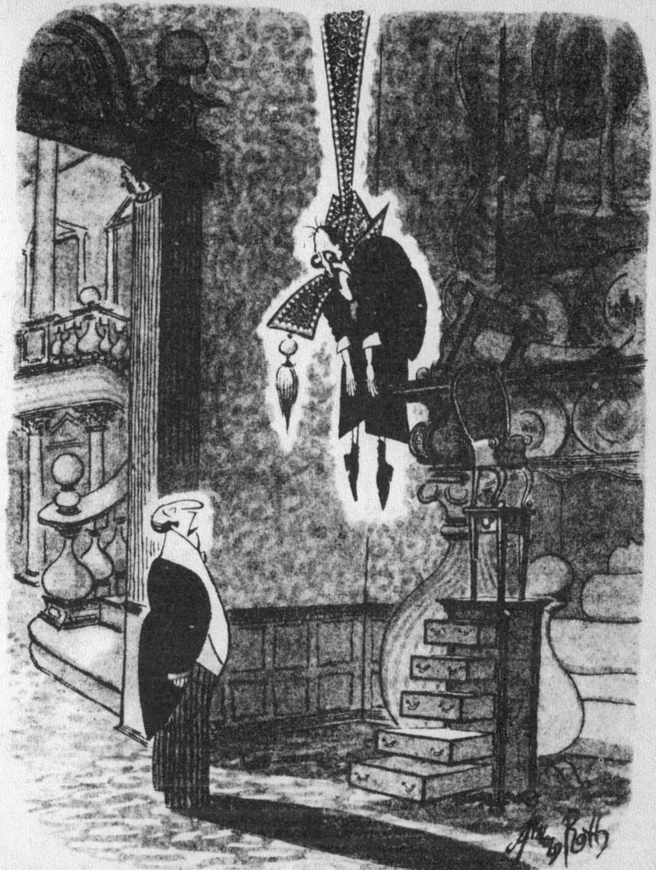

"You rang, sir?"

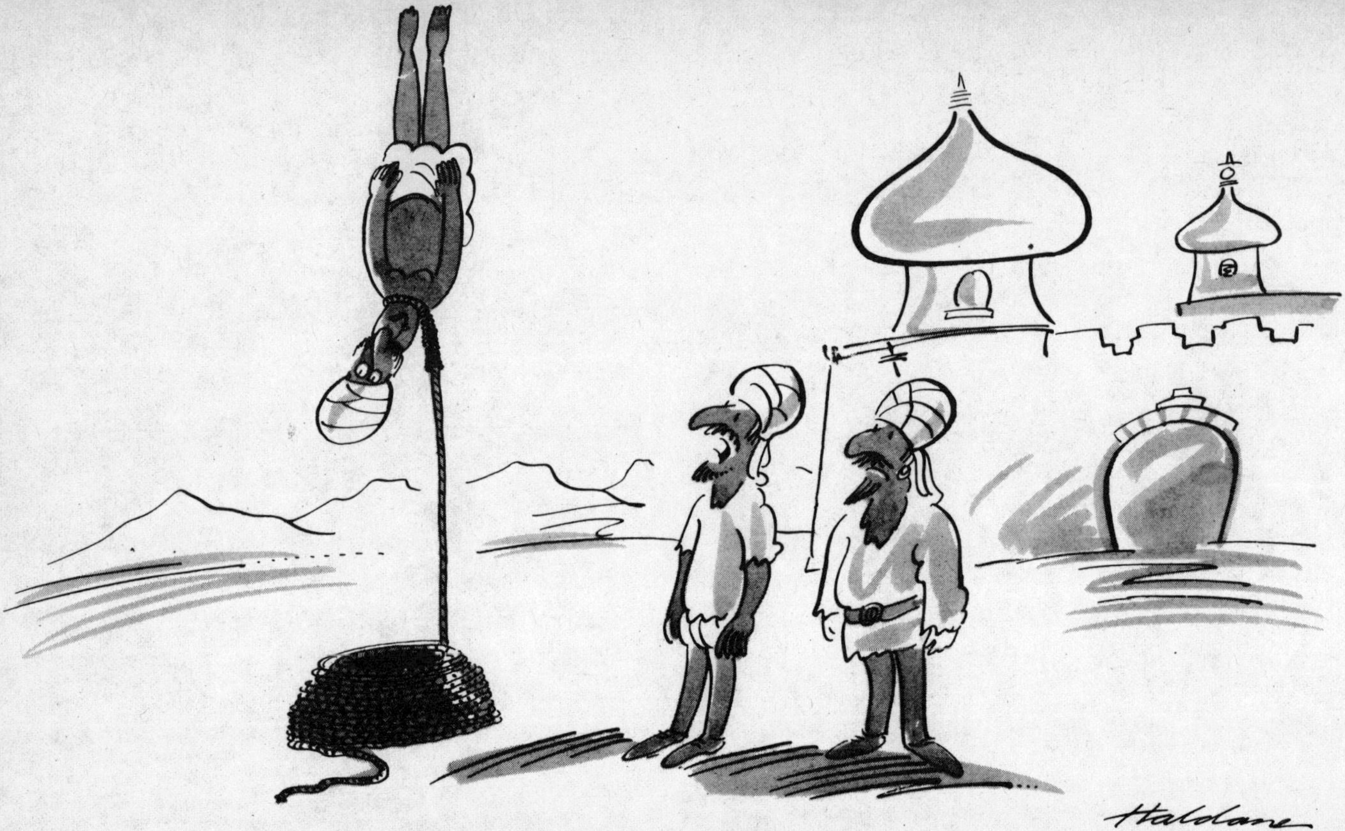

"It's sad, just when he was getting the hang of it."

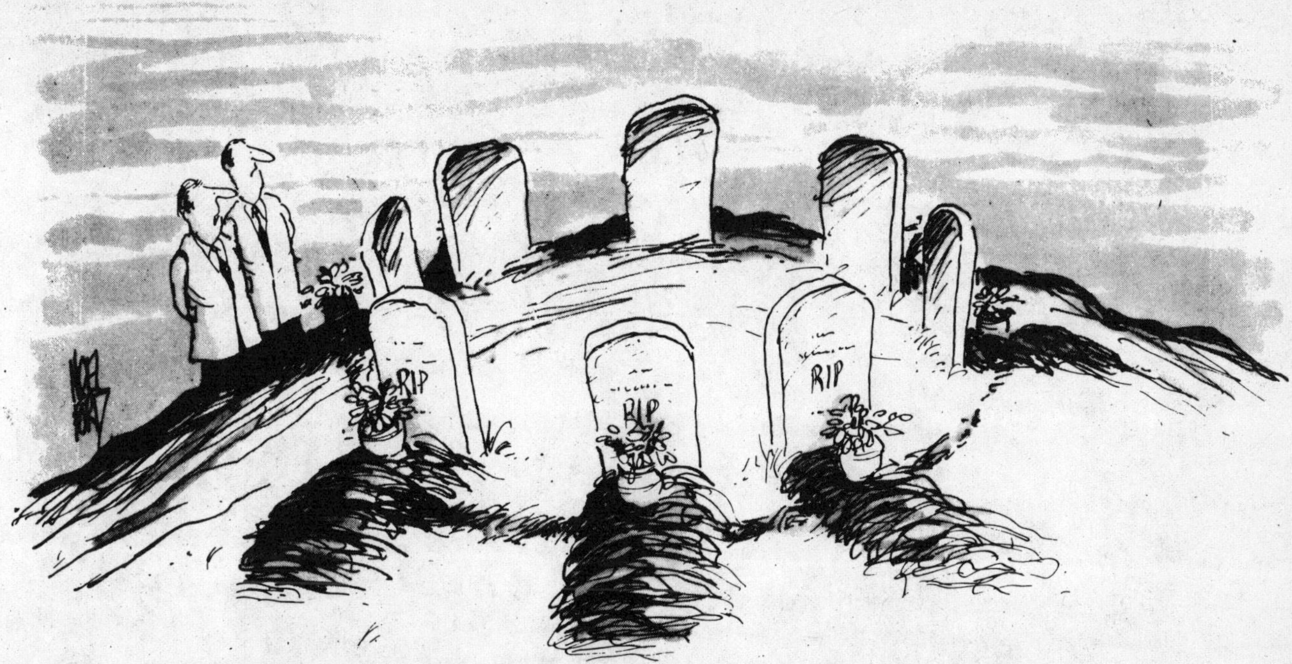

"Yes, they were one of the really great parachute teams."

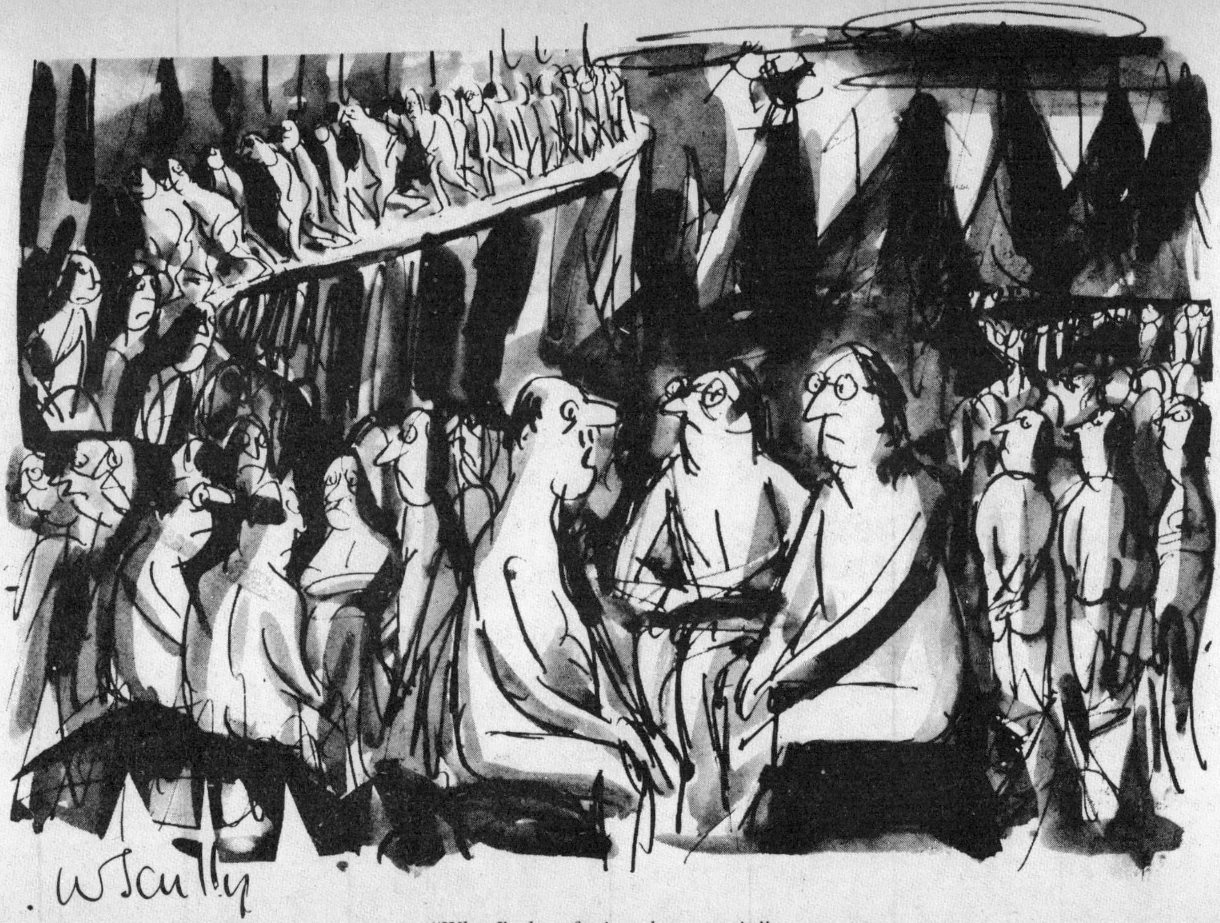

"What I'm here for is no longer a sin."

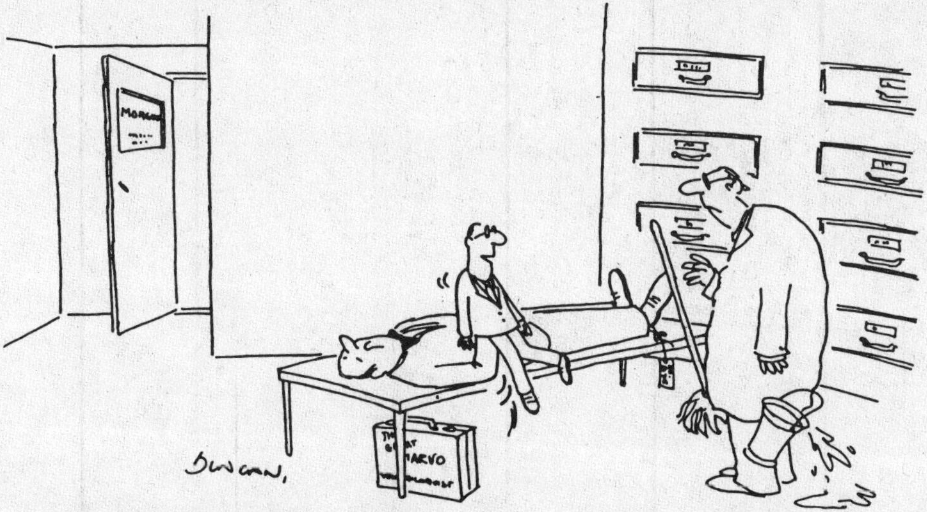

"Don't be alarmed. These muscular spasms are quite normal and occur frequently for some time after death."

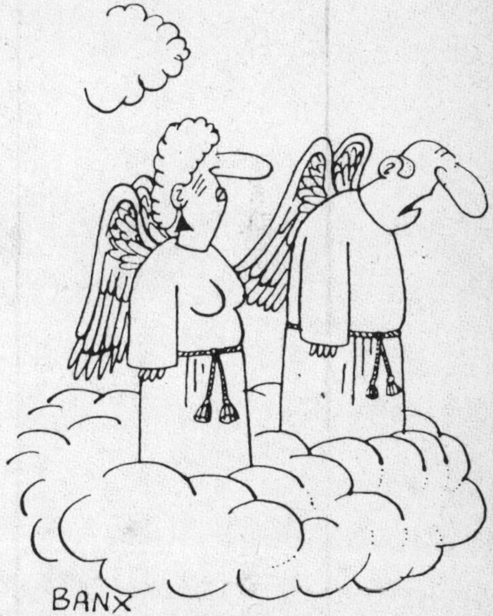

"I think my wife's becoming suspicious, Miss Dobson."

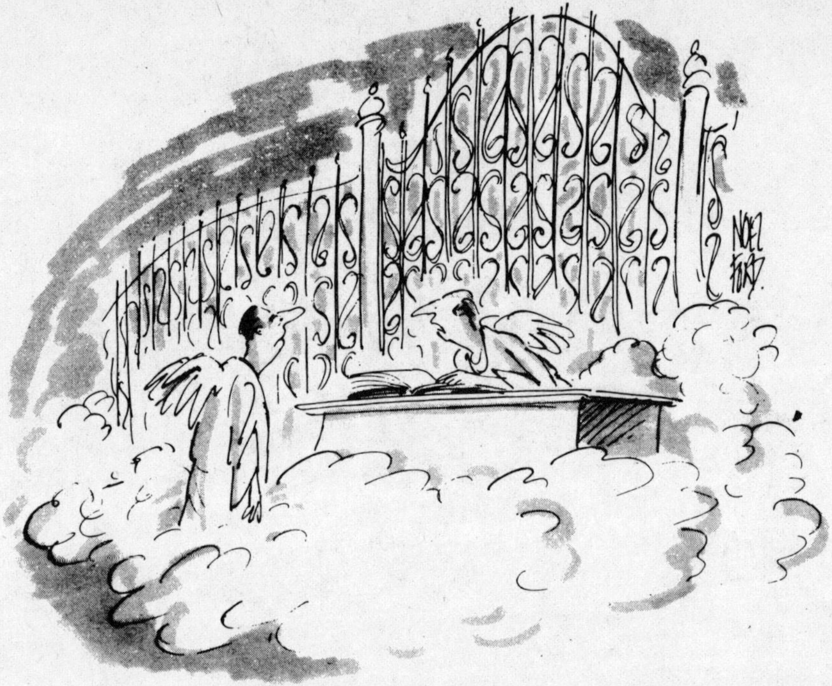

"Smoking or non-smoking?"

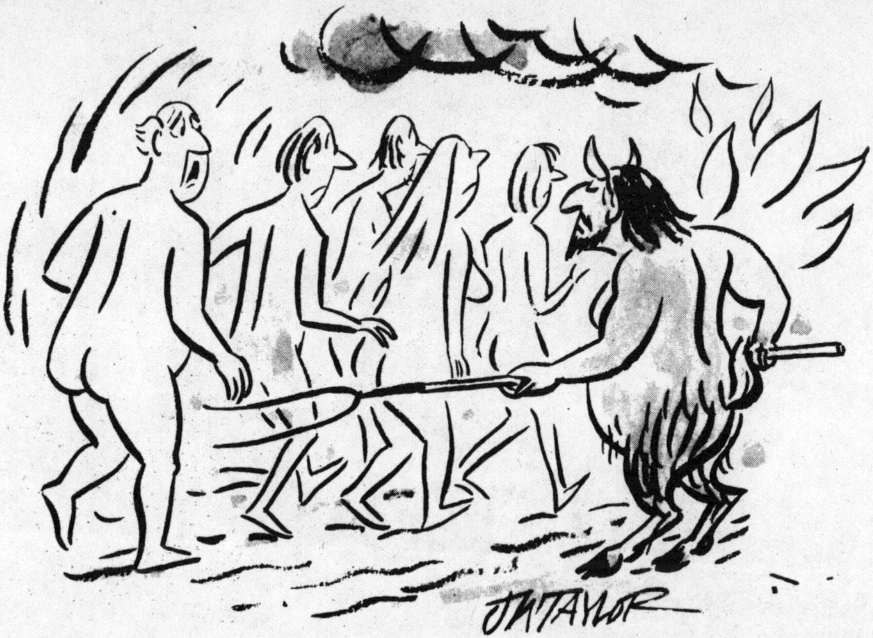

"There's been a terrible mistake – I was a tax avoider."

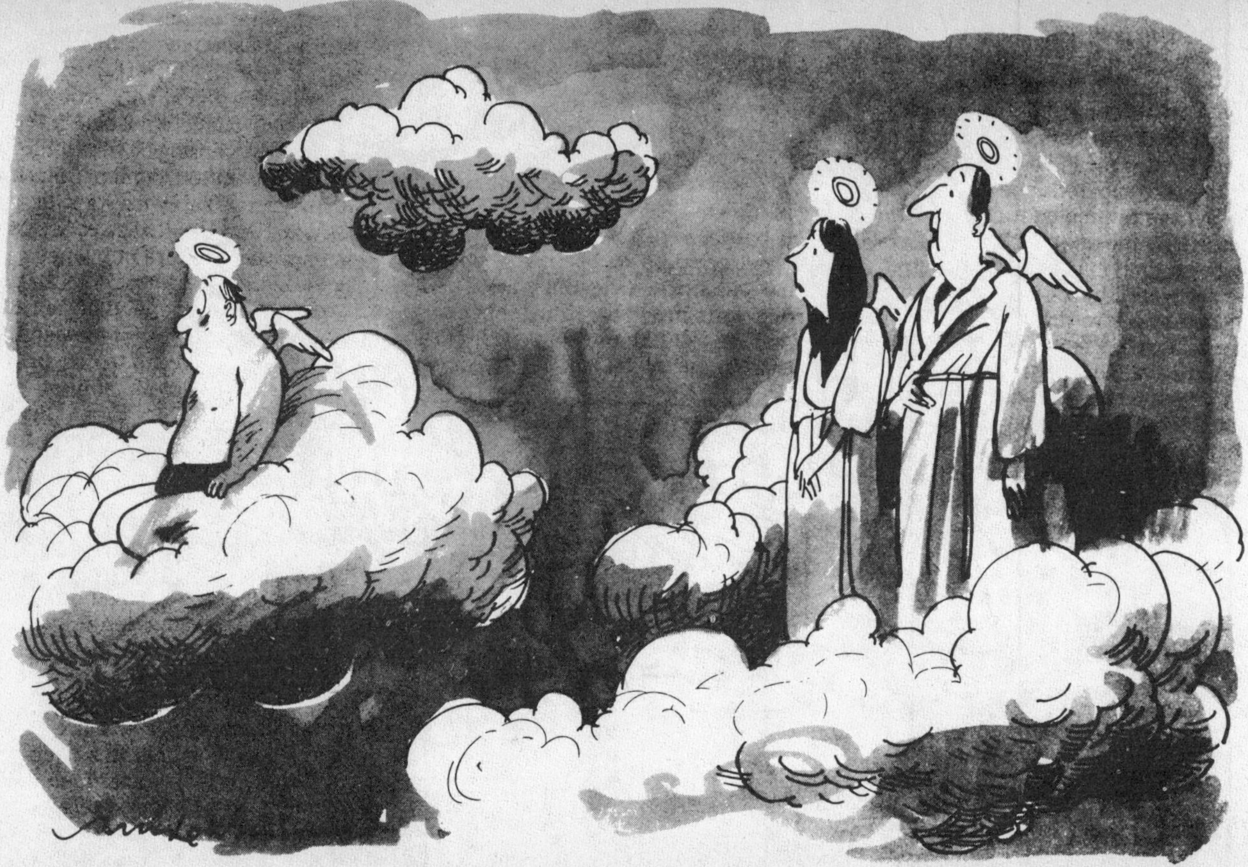

"It's a rather sad case really – he wanted to be remembered for his famous last words but all he said was 'It's not bad once you're in!'"

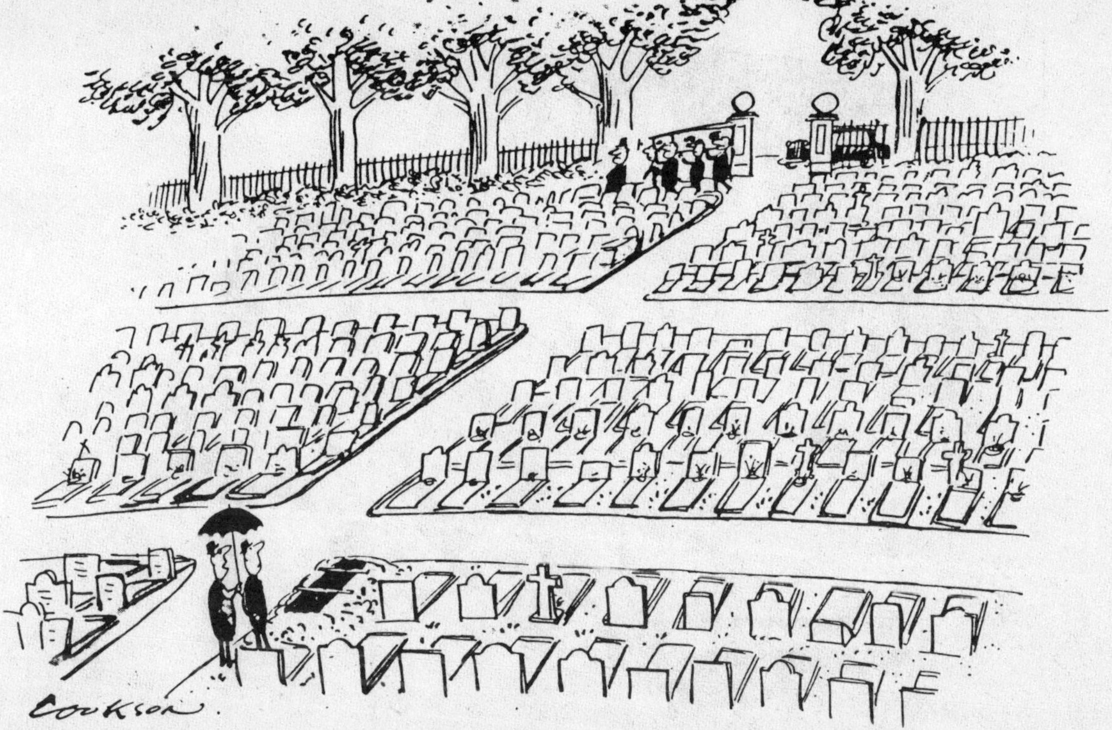

"Yes, he always liked to go the pretty way round."

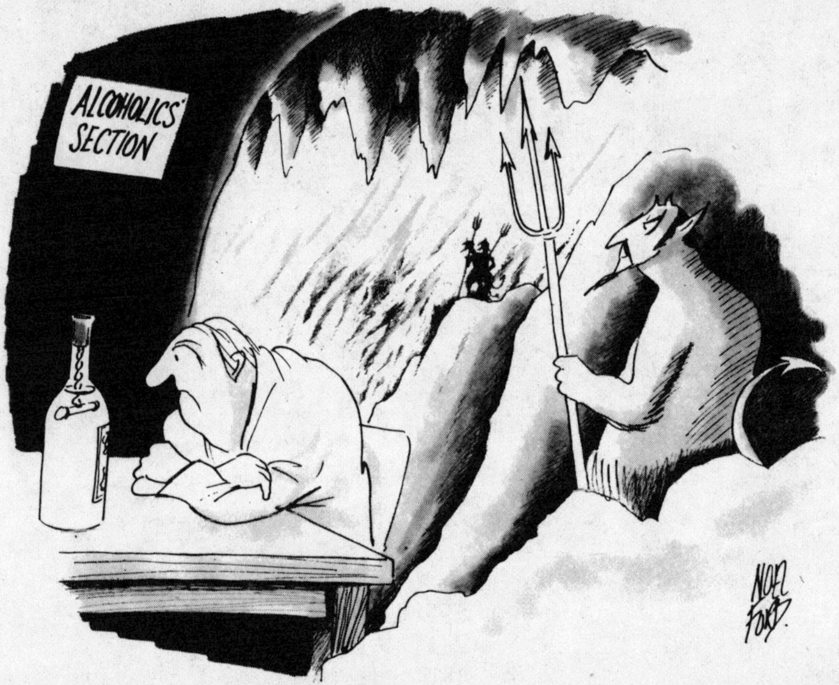
ALCOHOLICS' SECTION
NOEL FORD

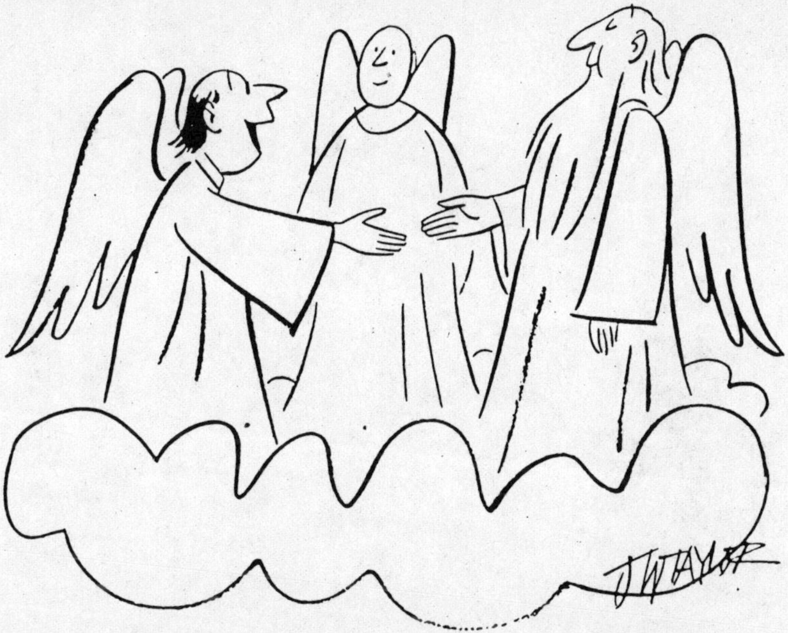

"Not the Amminadab that begat Nahshon that begat Salmon that begat Boaz that begat Obed that begat Jesse that begat David?"

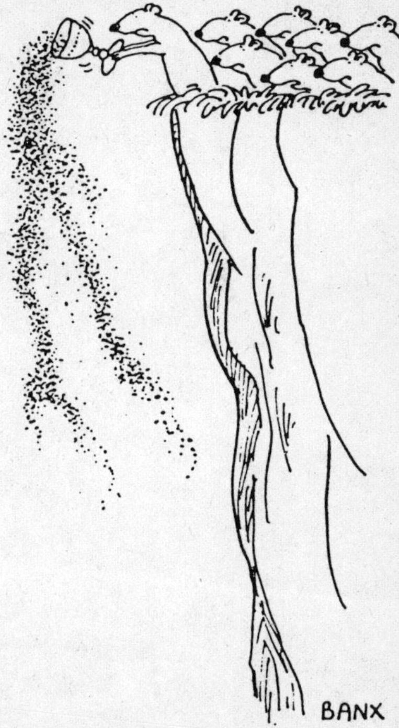

"It's the way he would have wanted it."

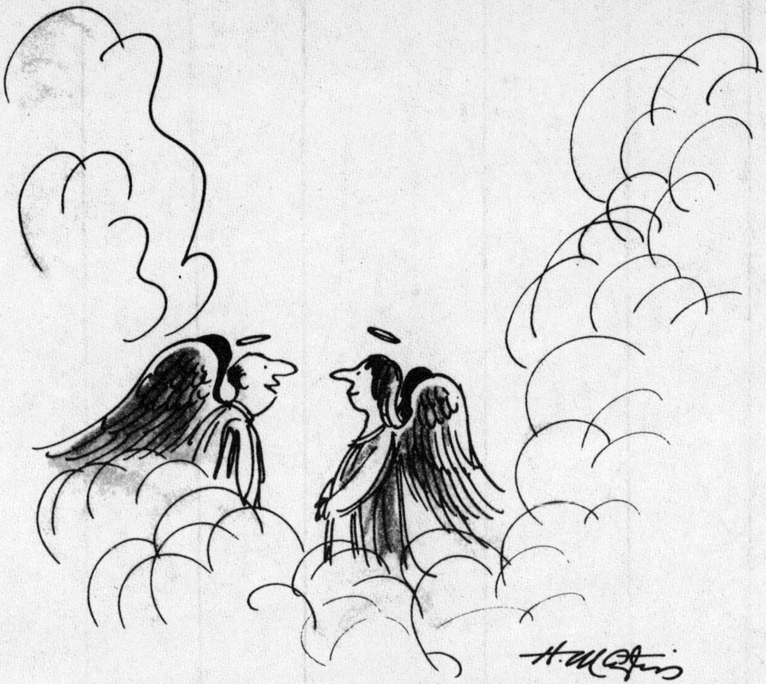

"We're having a celebrity roast tonight for Mark Twain."

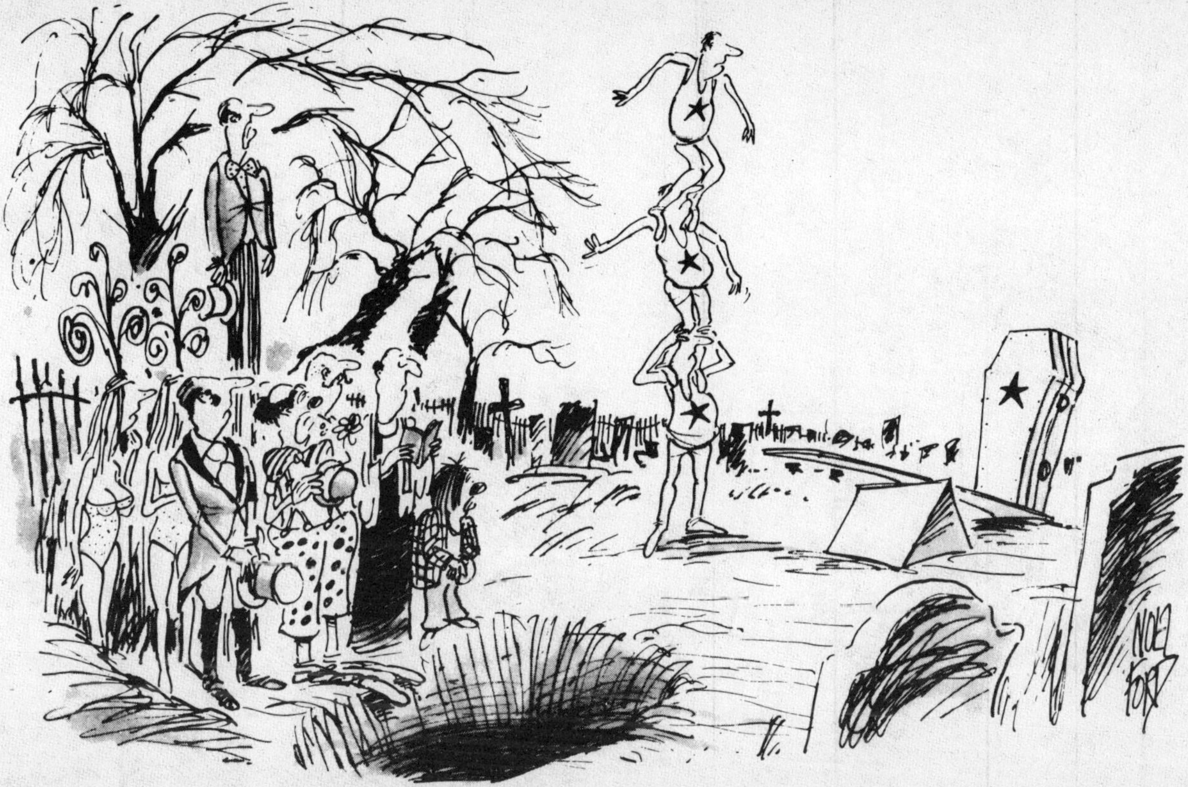
NOEL FORD

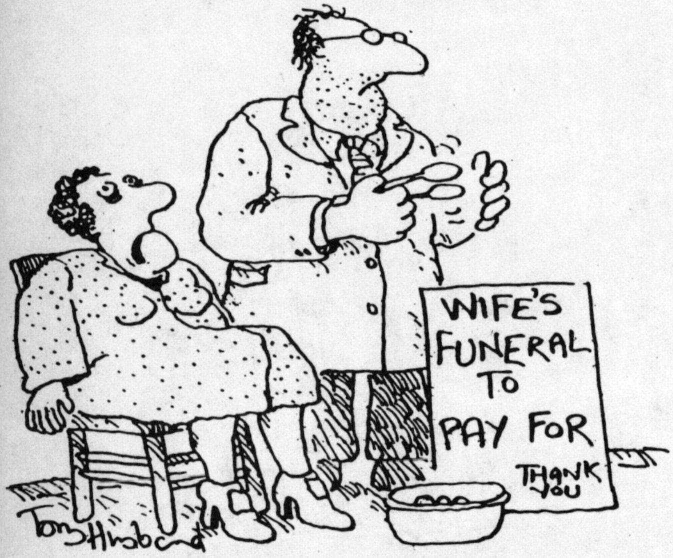
WIFE'S
FUNERAL
TO
PAY FOR
THANK
YOU
Tony Husband

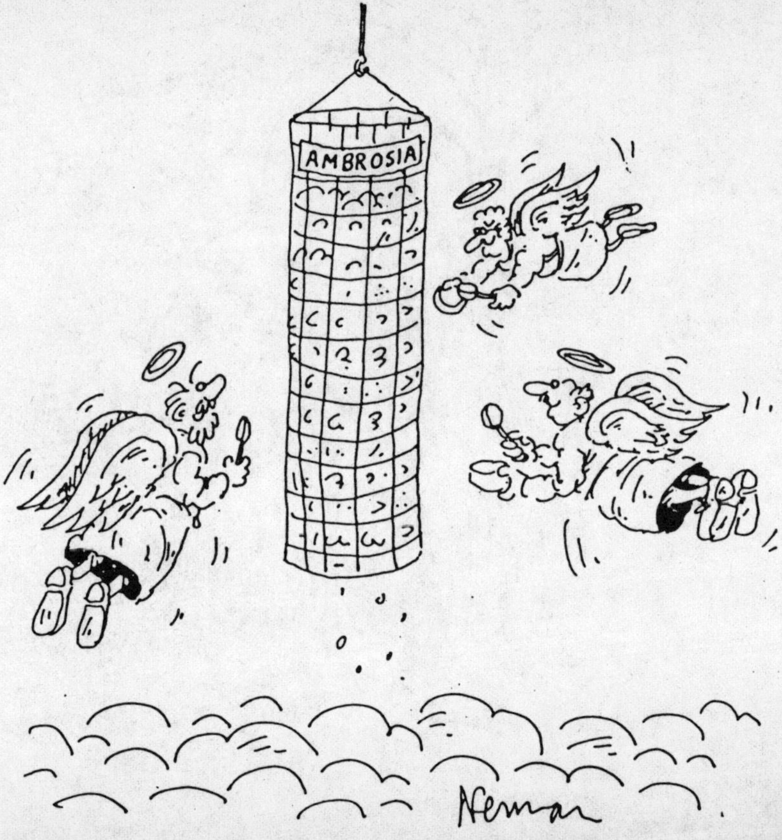
AMBROSIA
Newman

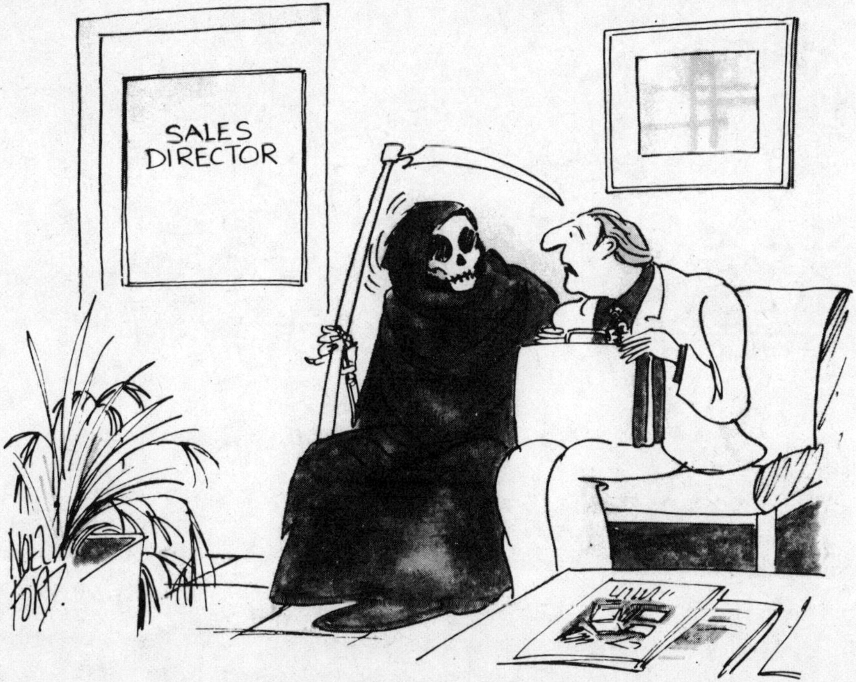

"Would you mind awfully if I went in first?"

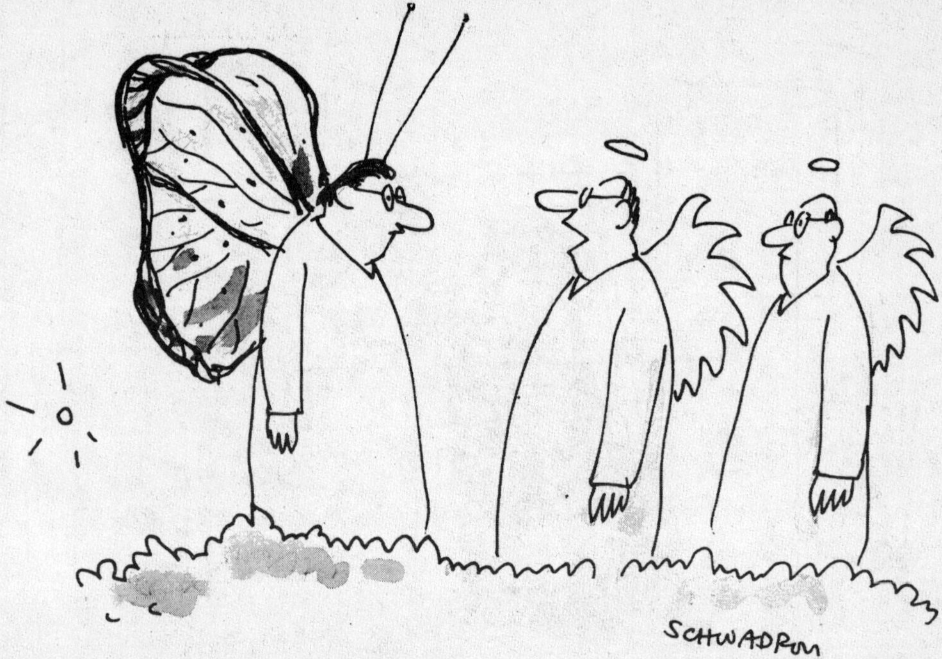

"We're sorry, Beardsley, but the consensus up here is that you're an impostor."